Necropolises of New Orleans I

A TRAVEL PHOTO ART BOOK

LAINE CUNNINGHAM

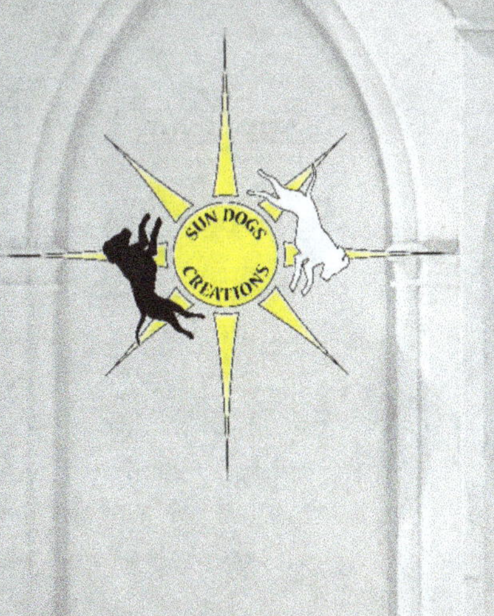

Necropolises of New Orleans I
A Travel Photo Art Book

Published by Sun Dogs Creations
Changing the World One Book at a Time
ISBN: 9781946732217

Softcover Edition

Cover Design by Angel Leya

Introduction

Since the city of New Orleans is built on a swamp, the dead are enshrined above ground. Row upon row of crypts and mausoleums, each built with a different style, look very much like small neighborhoods. Filled with elaborate entryways, wrought iron fences, and decorative rooftop statues, the cemeteries have become known as Cities of the Dead.

In these cities you'll discover Greek Revival styling, ornate gates, marble steps, crypts made entirely of cast iron, and broad slabs of beautiful stones. Although the vaults are made necessary by frequent flooding, they also reflect the heritage of French and Spanish colonists, who were accustomed to seeing these types of burials in their homelands.

These photos were taken at Greenwood Cemetery & Mausoleum, St. Louis Cemetery No. 2, and Saint Patrick Cemetery No. 2. They have been reproduced at the size of a standard cellphone screen to replicate a visit to these beautiful, touching, and meditative places. Just as you would with a phone, at times you'll need to rotate the book to view the picture.

Discover history, spirituality, and deeply resonant meaning in *Necropolises of New Orleans I*.

CAPITOLIUM

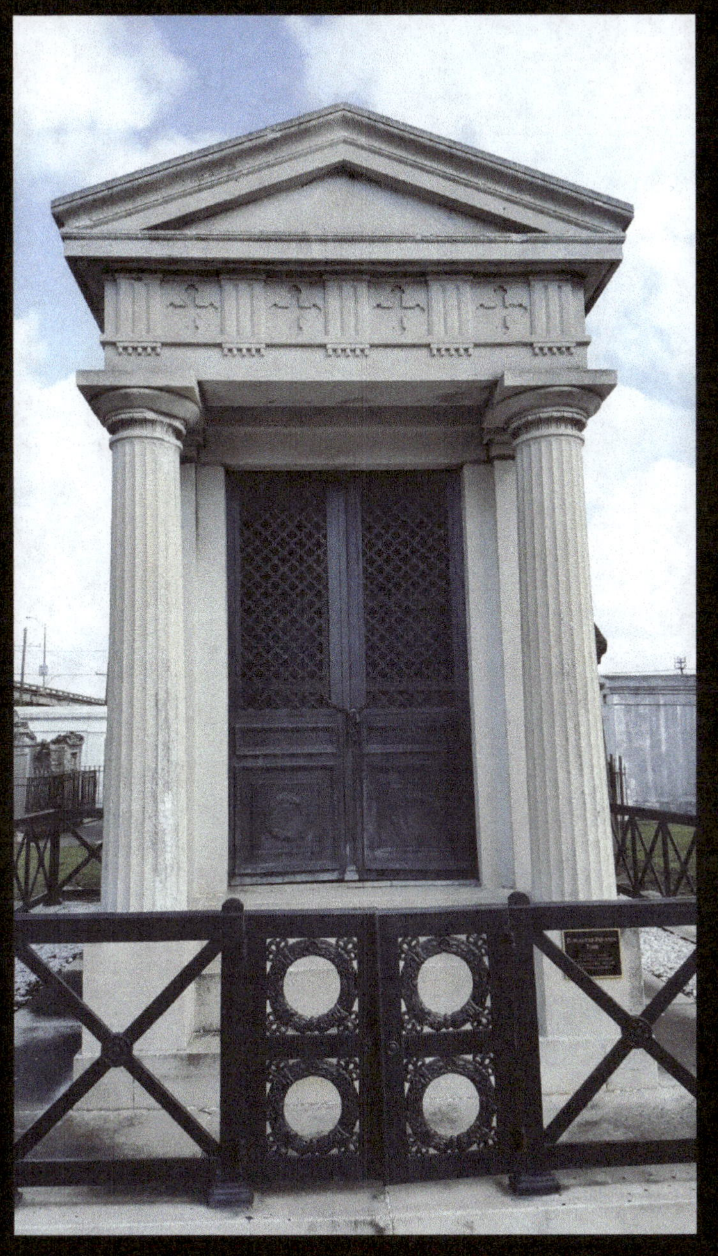

ALL IN A ROW

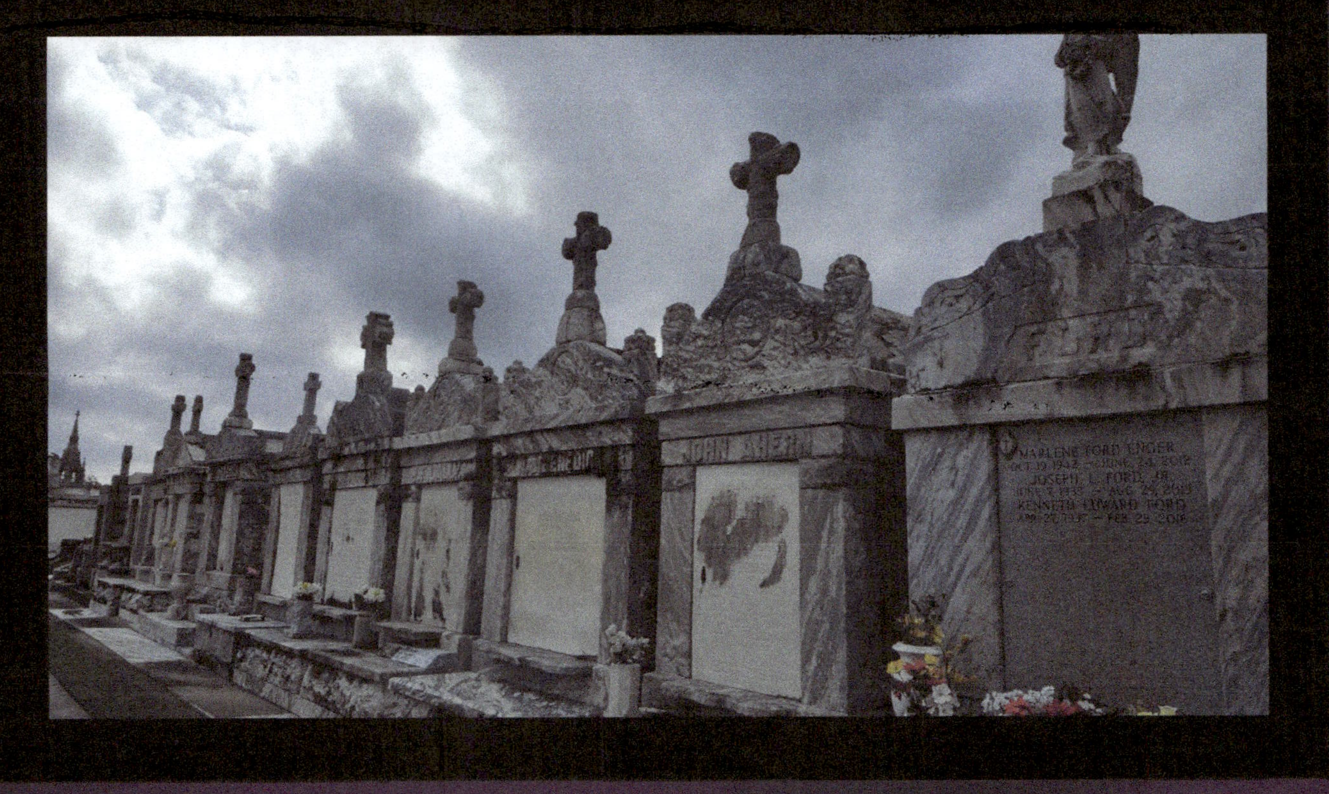
MARLENE FORD UNGER
OCT 19 1942 - JUNE 24 2012
JOSEPH L FORD JR
JUNE 2 1935 - AUG 24 2013
KENNETH EDWARD FORD
APR 22 1937 - FEB 29 2016
JOHN AHERN

BISECT

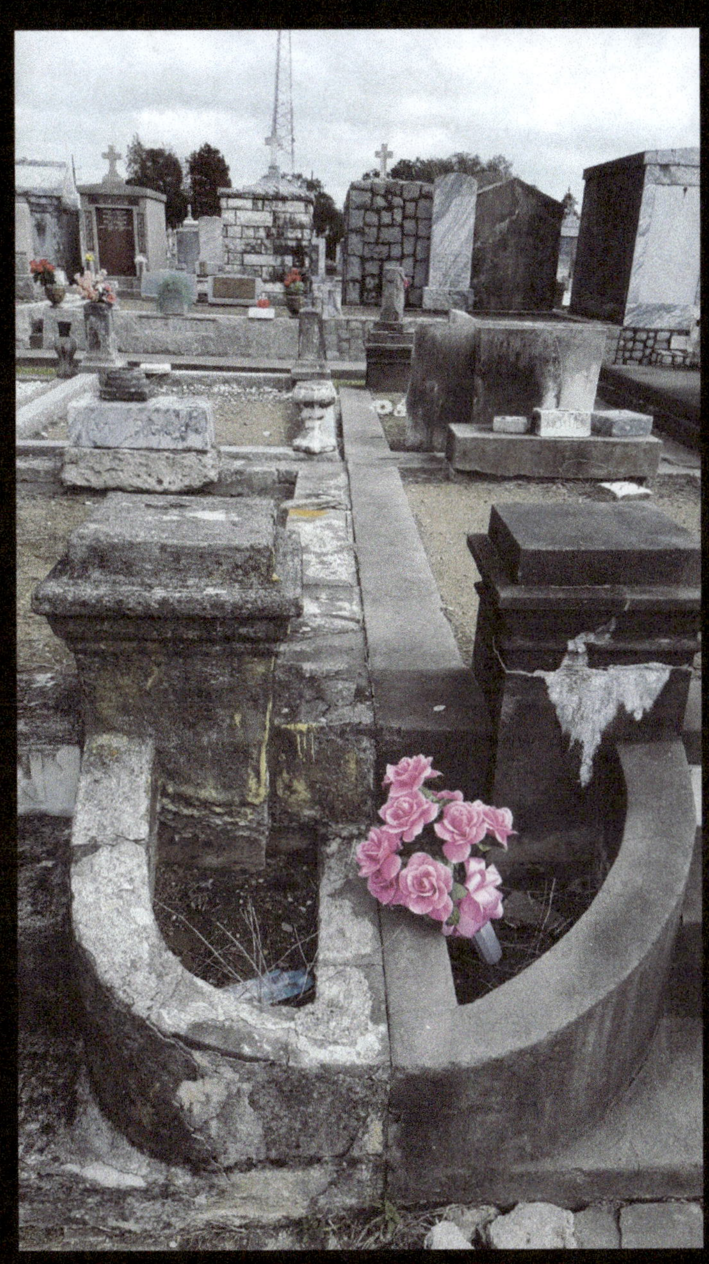

CITYSCAPE

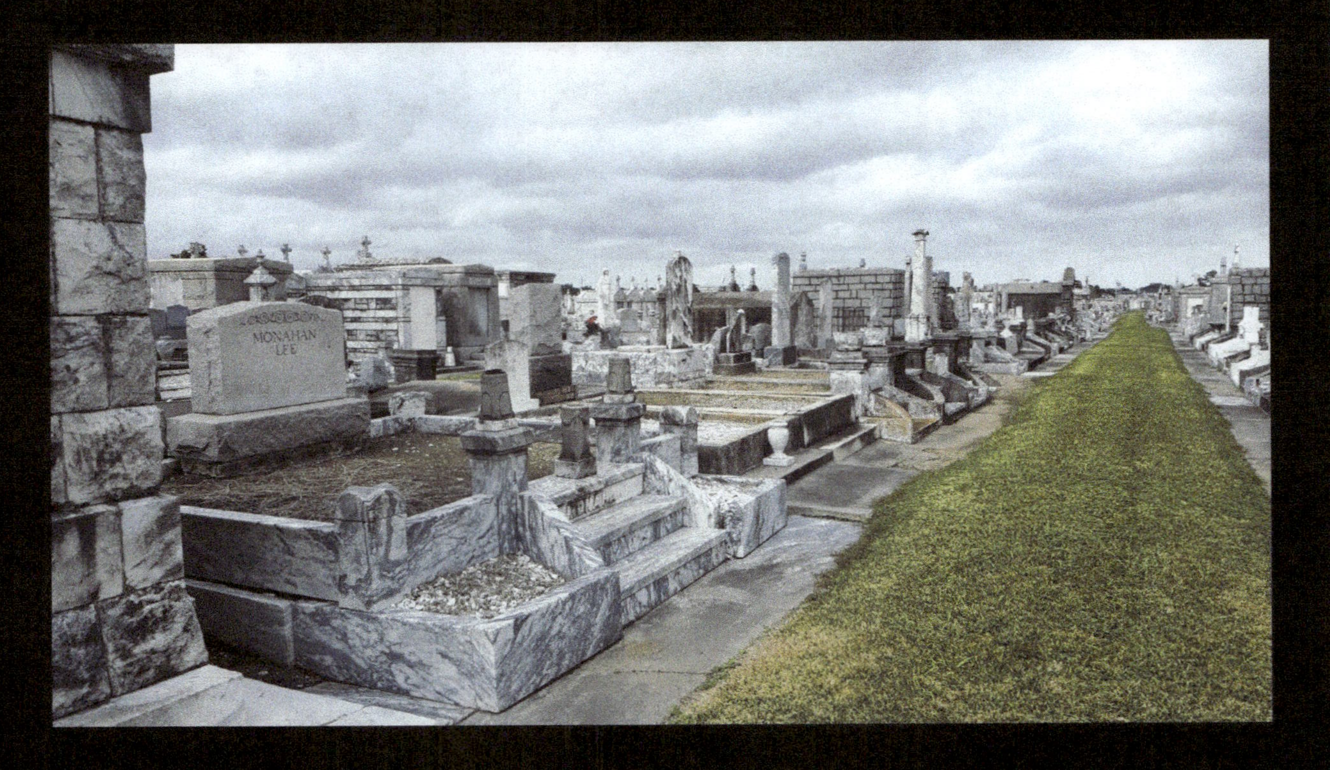

MONAHAN
LEE

ELVES

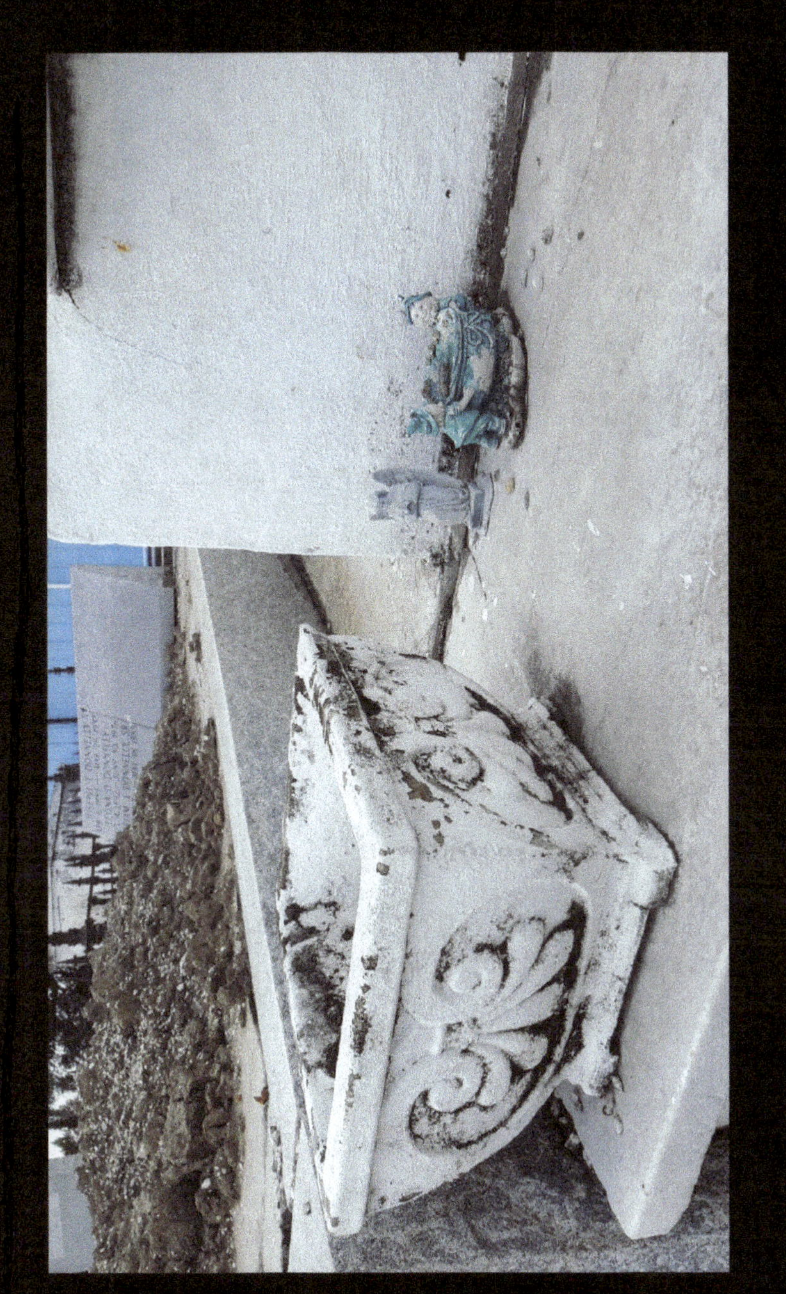

GATEWAY

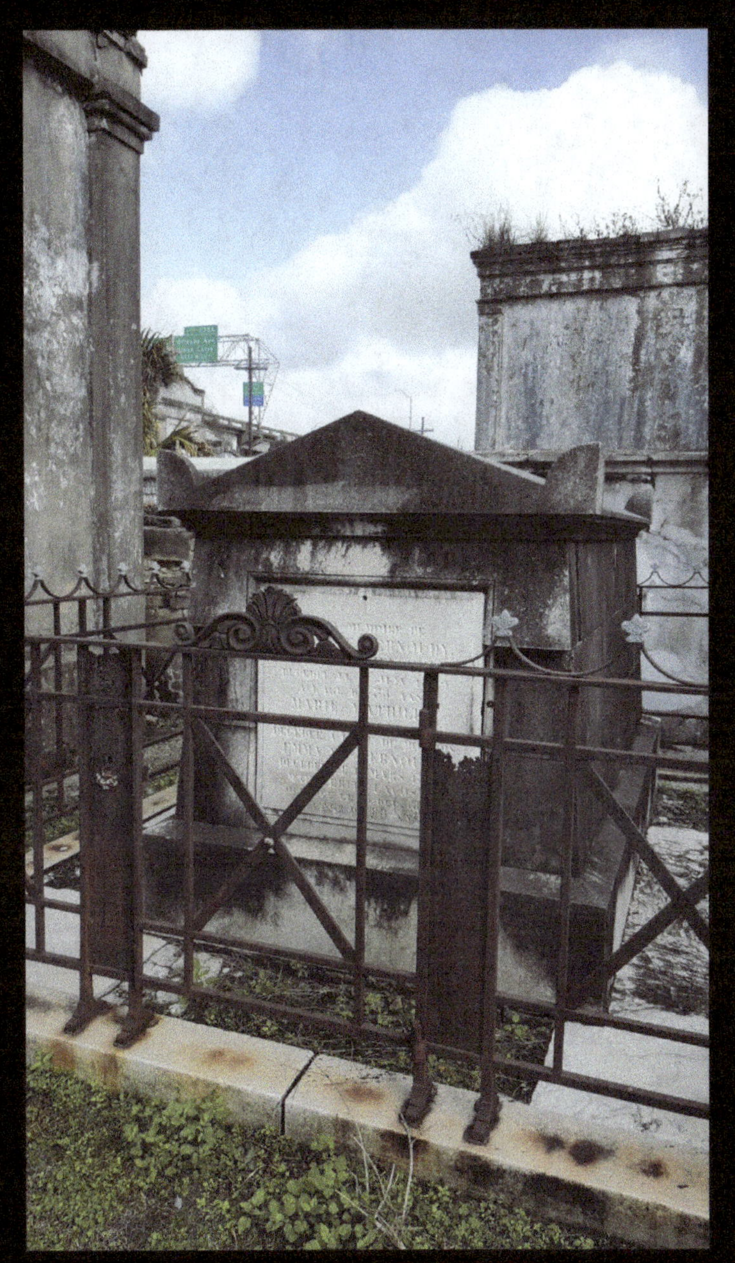

ALL GRAY

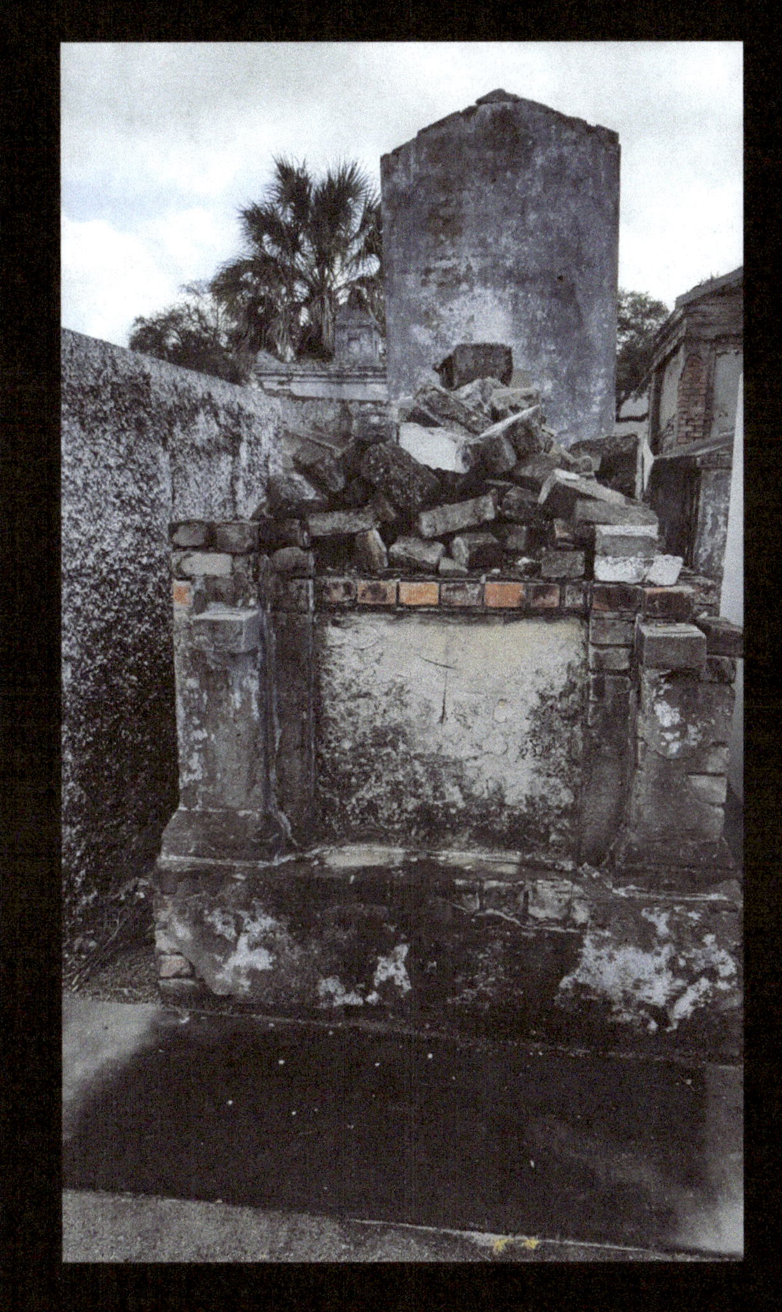

FOLIOLE

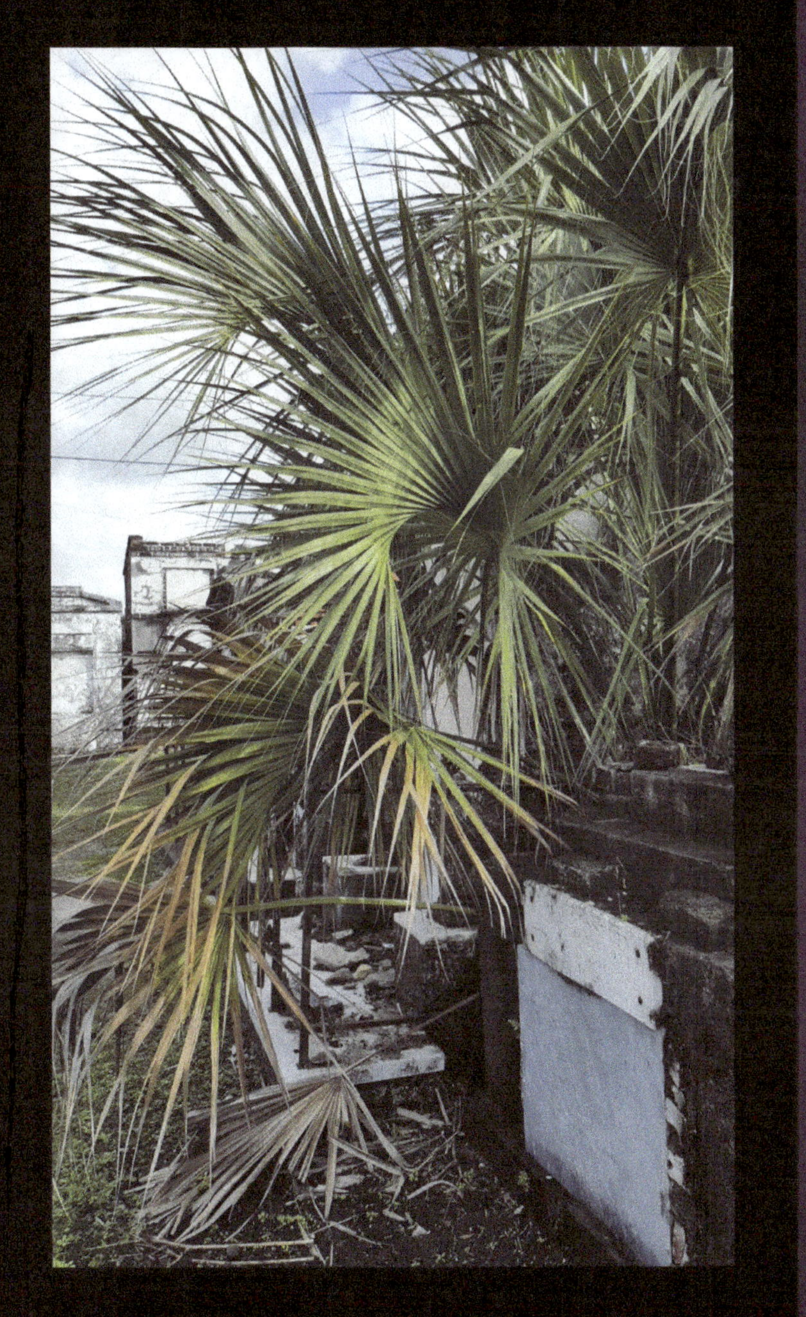

LOST IN THE RUBBLE

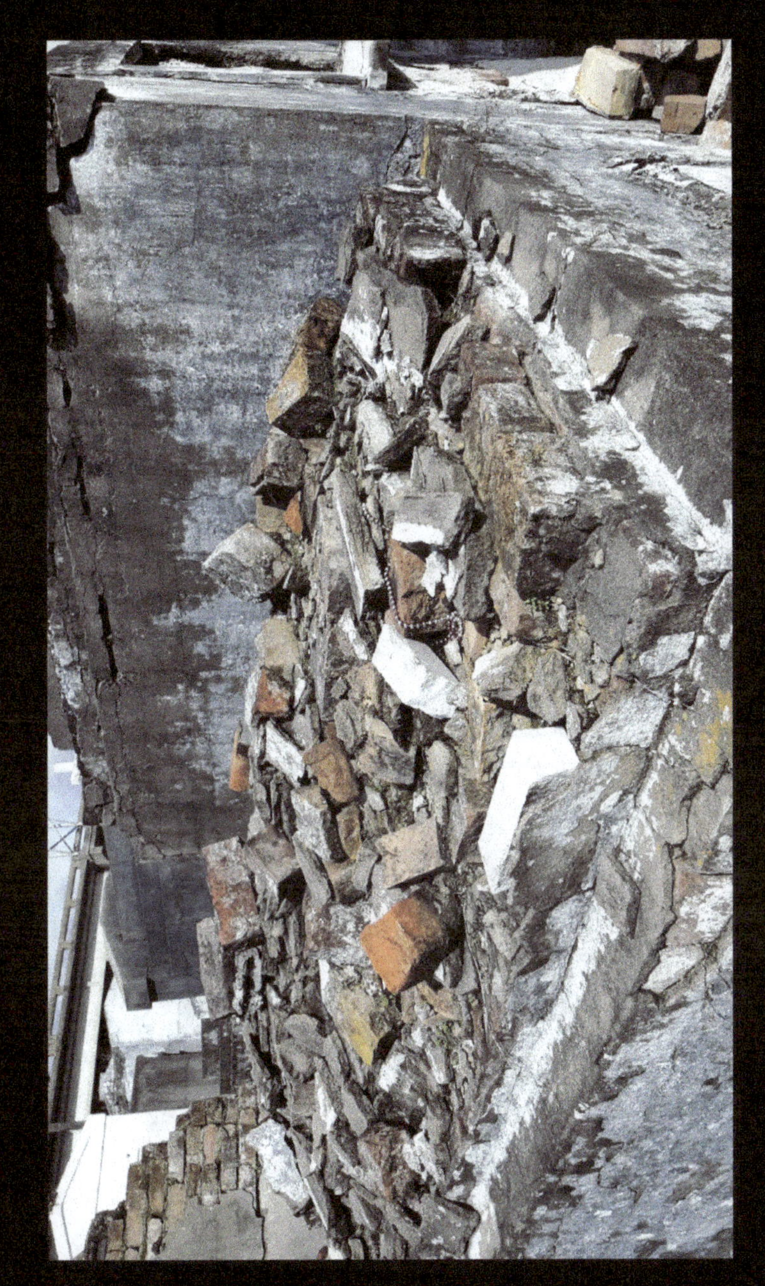

SALOY 1924

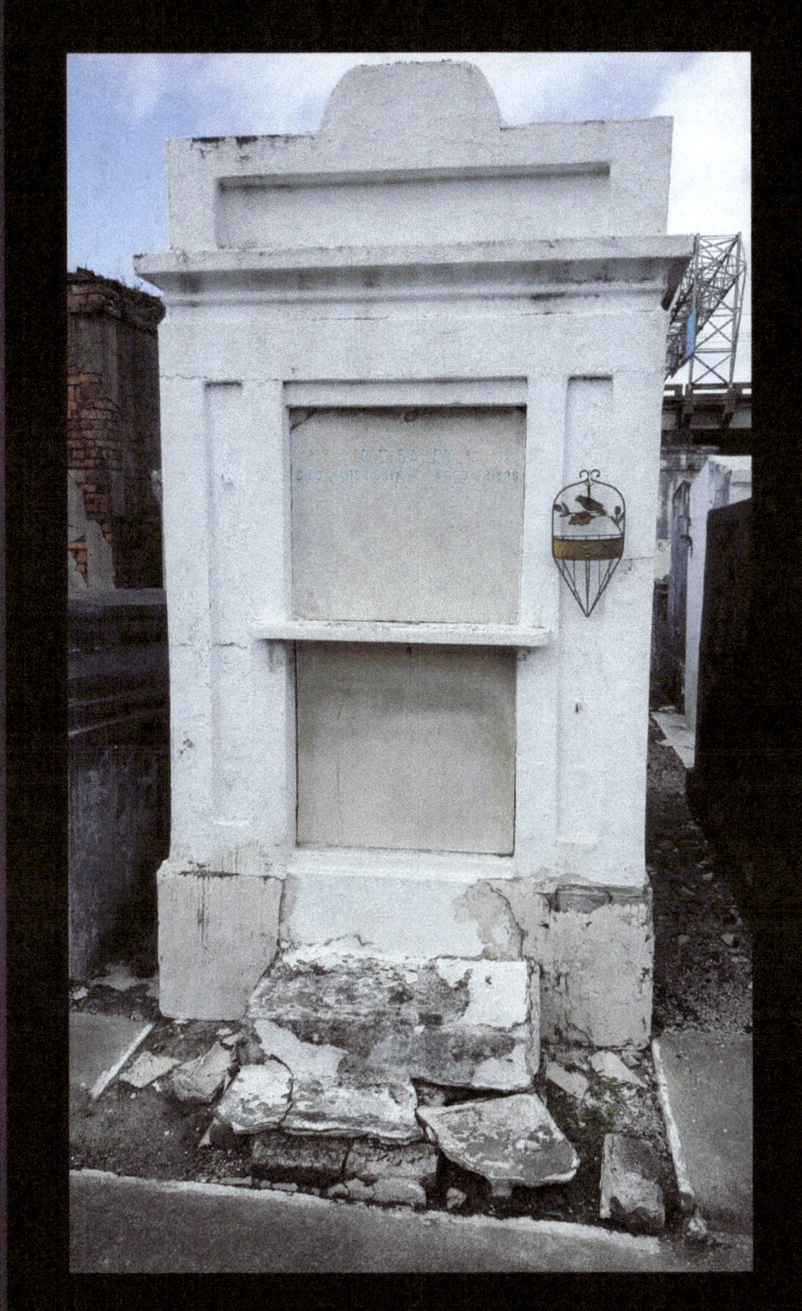

PALISADE

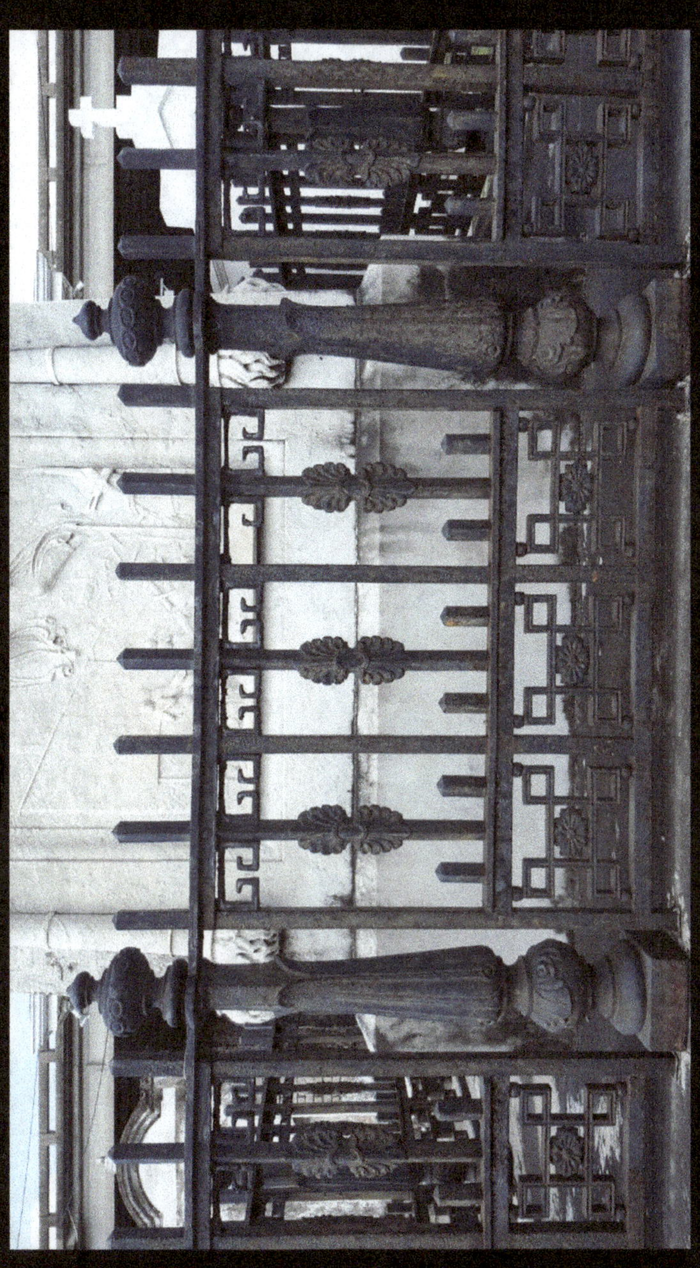

SUNKEN STELE

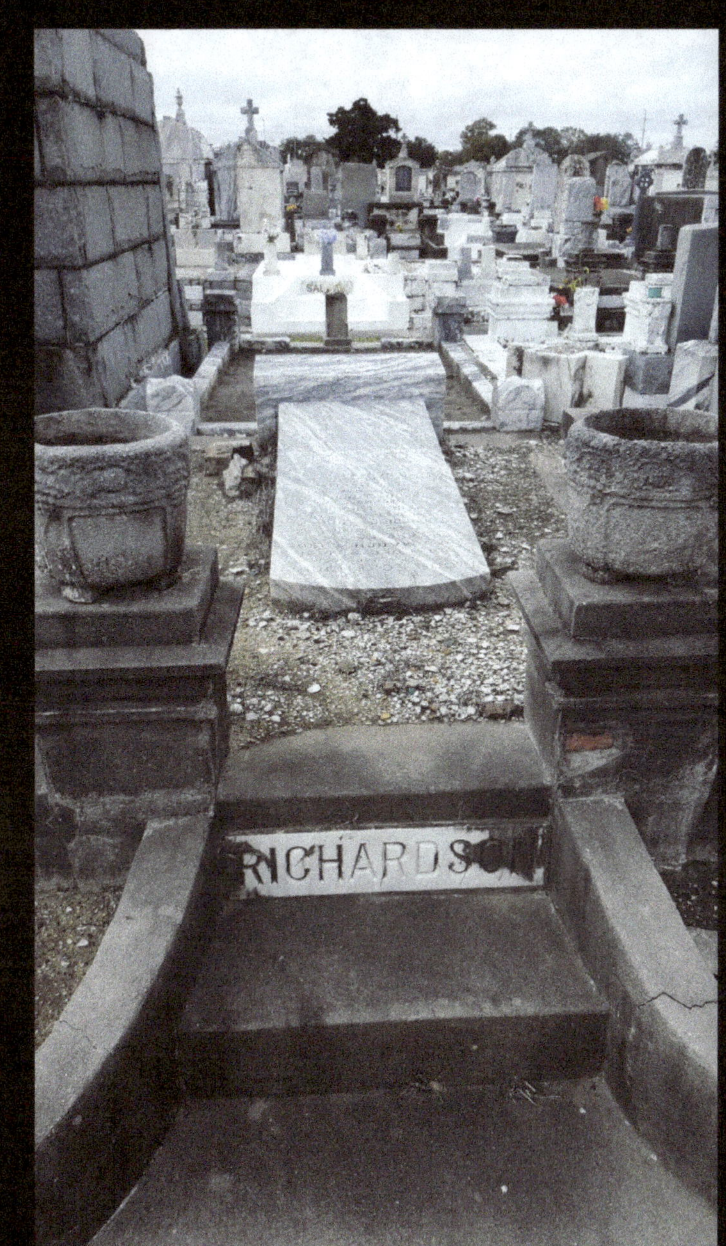
RICHARDSON

UNDERWORLD

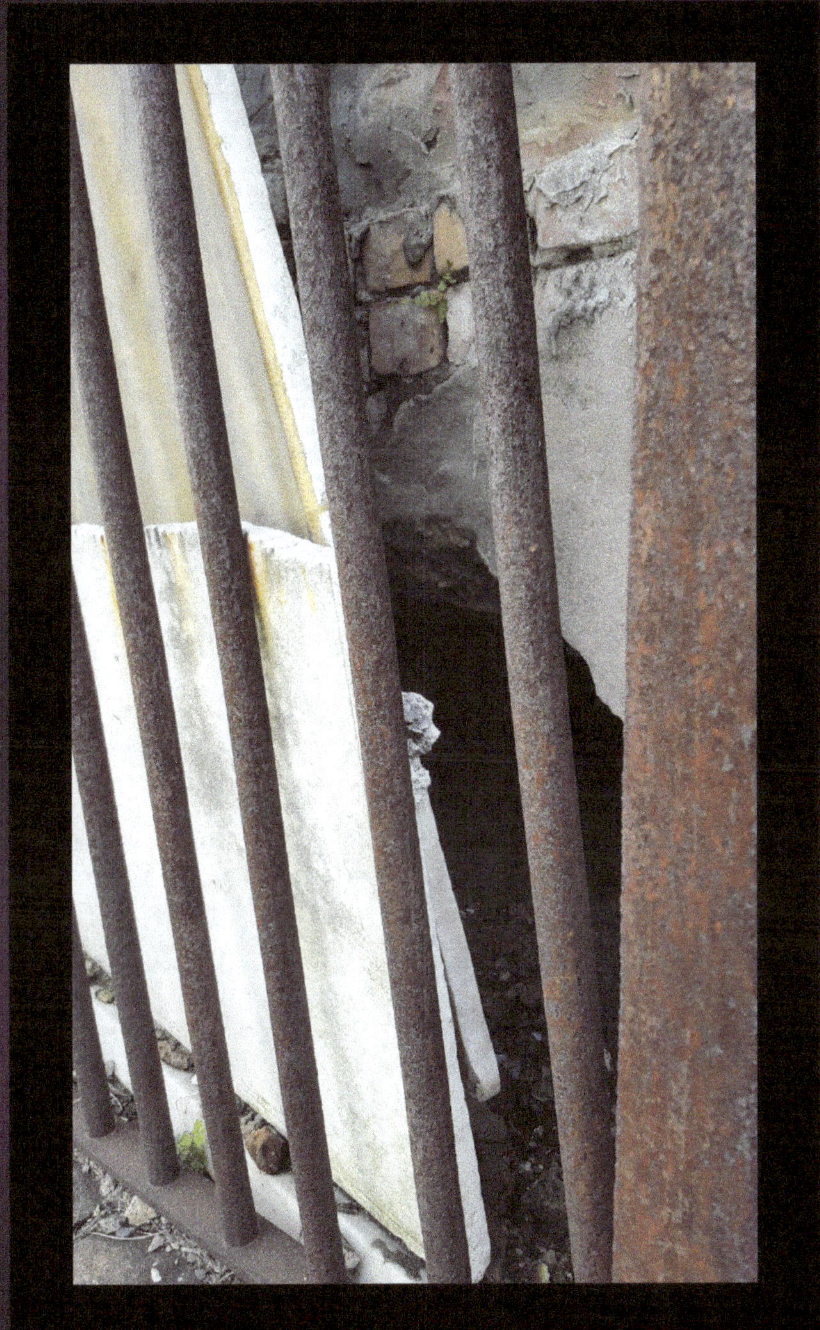

GEOMETRY

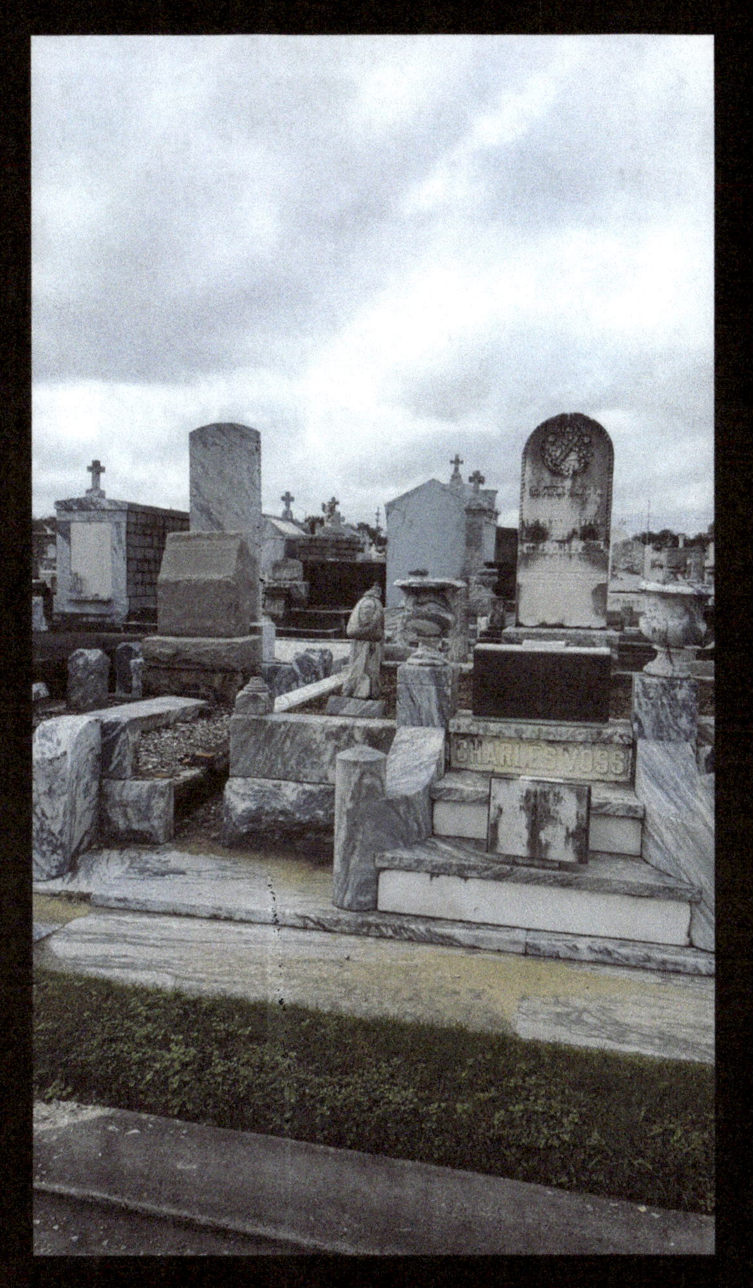
CHARLES VOSS

BRASCO'S HOLIDAY

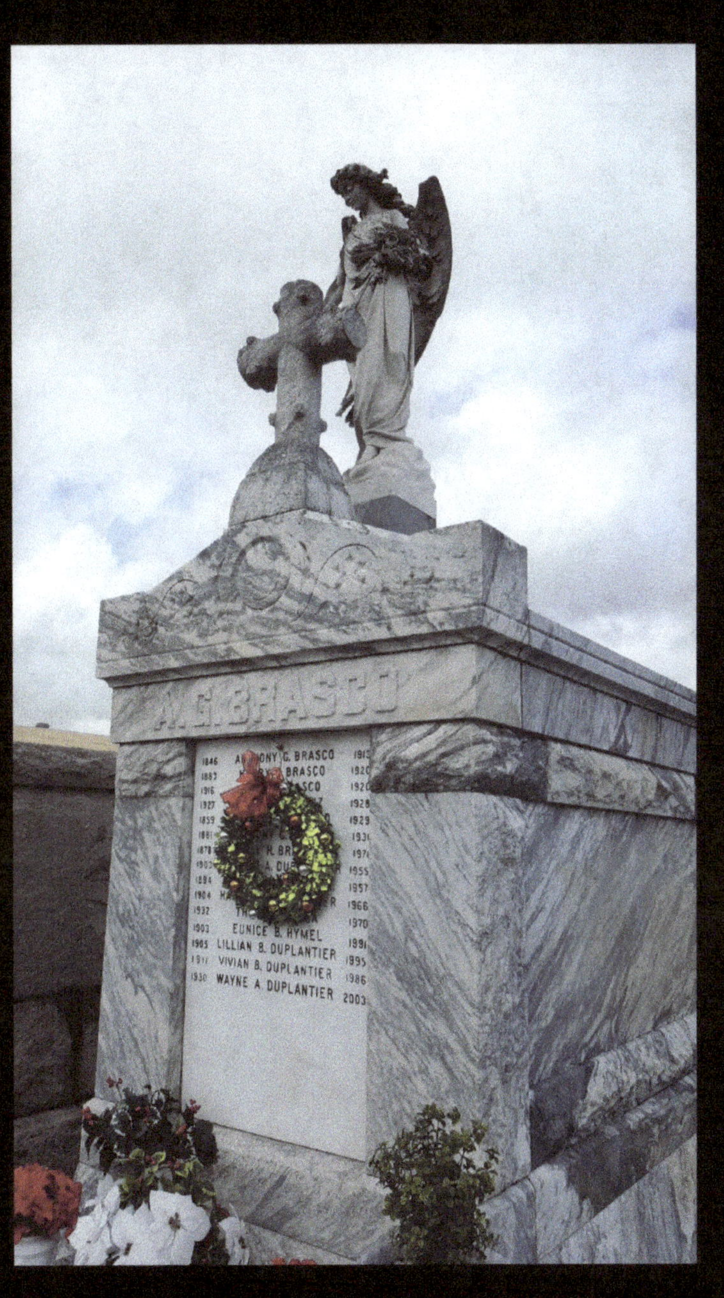
A. G. BRASCO
1846 ANTHONY G. BRASCO 1915
1883 MARY B. BRASCO 1920
1916 BRASCO 1920
1927 1928
1859 1929
1881 1930
1878 BR 1974
1903 A. DU 1955
1894 1957
1904 1966
1932 1970
1903 EUNICE B. HYMEL
1905 LILLIAN B. DUPLANTIER 1991
1911 VIVIAN B. DUPLANTIER 1995
1930 WAYNE A. DUPLANTIER 1986
2003

CUL-DE-SAC

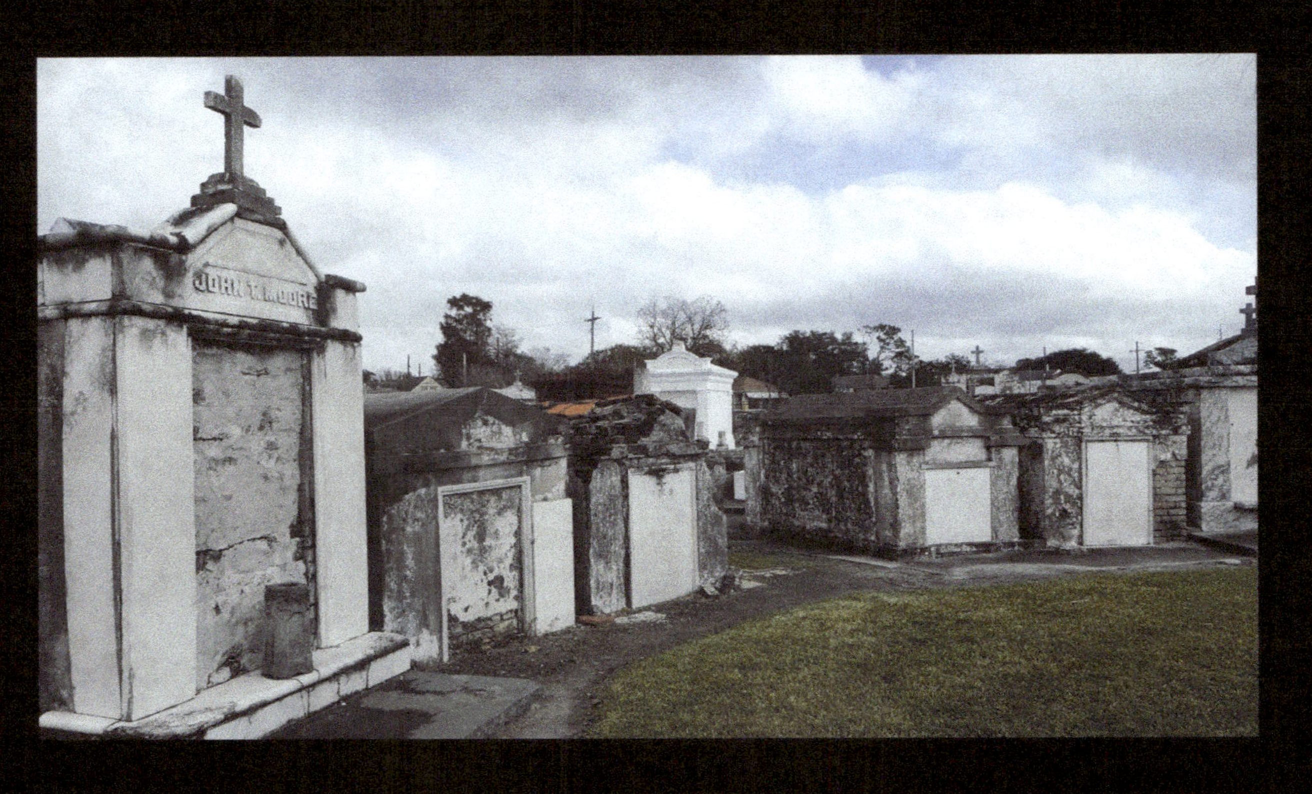
JOHN T. MOORE

KING EDWARD, QUEEN ALICE

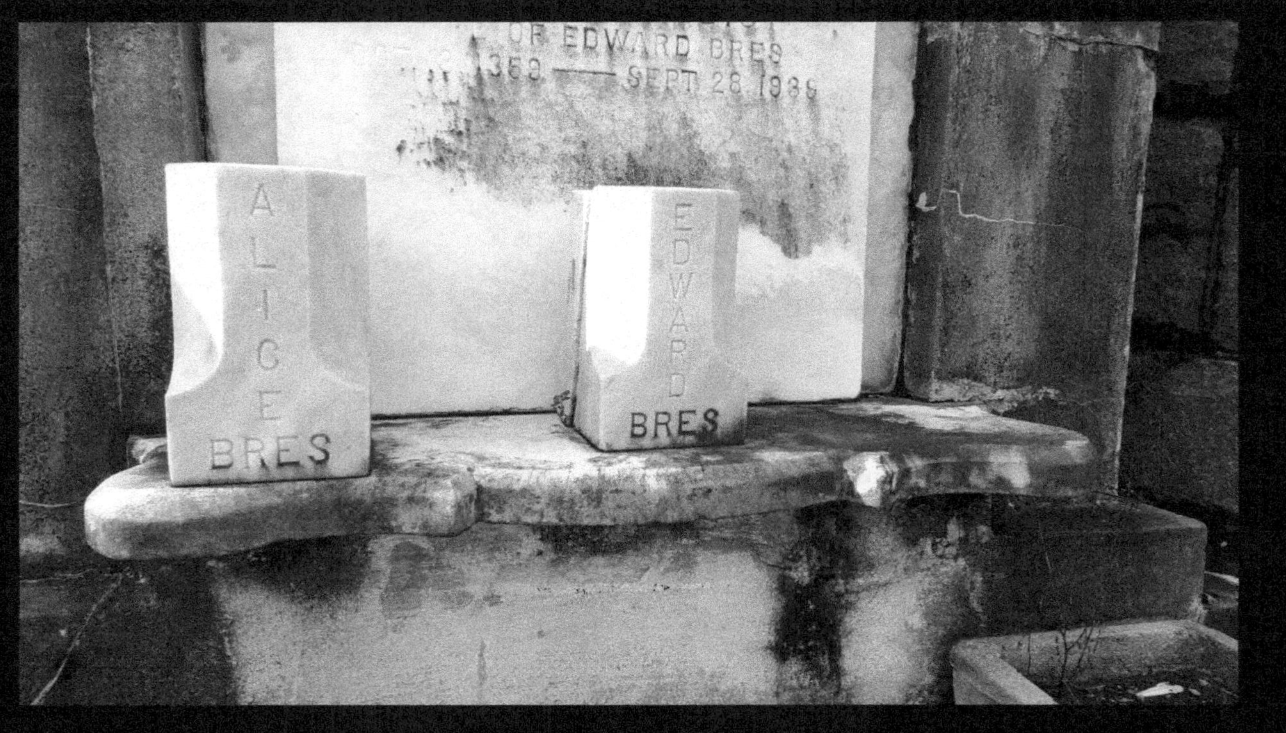
OF EDWARD BRES
1359 — SEPT 28 1939
ALICE
BRES
EDWARD
BRES

THE HOUSE OF ORANGE

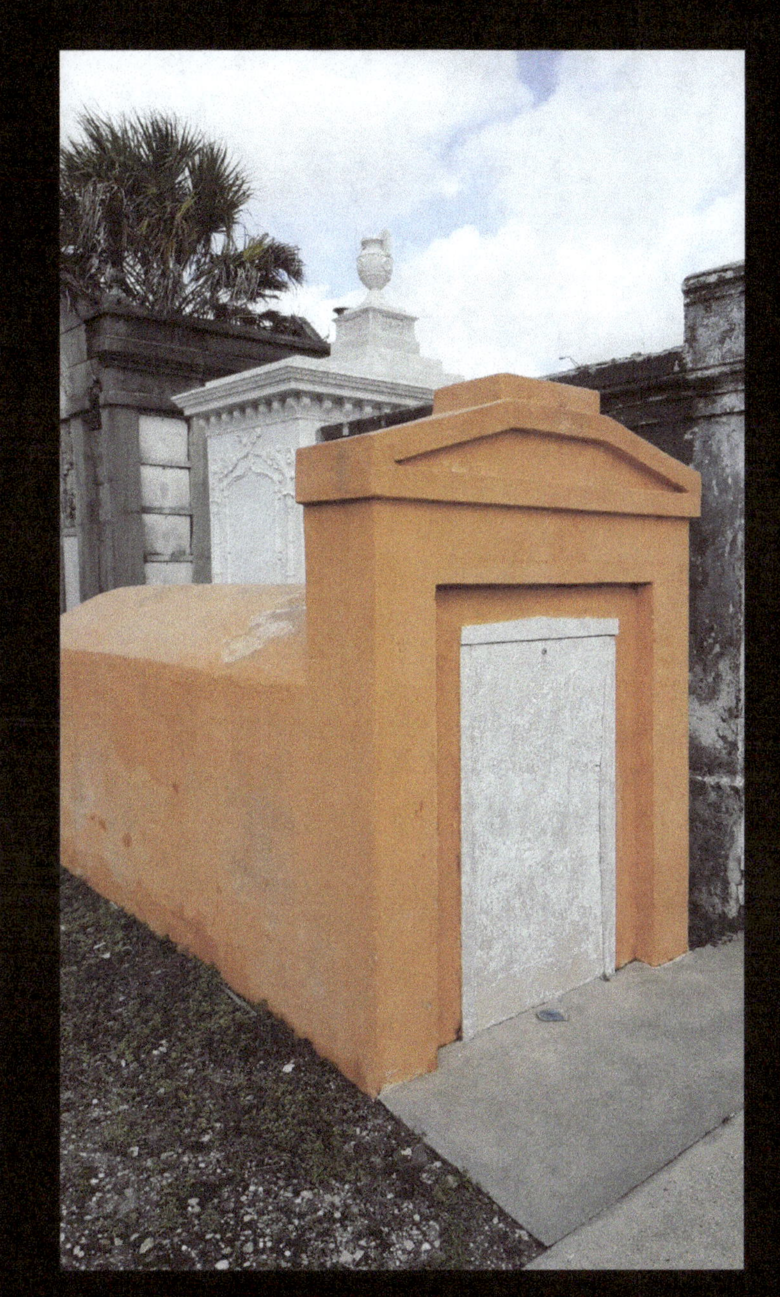

ST. PAUL'S GYRE

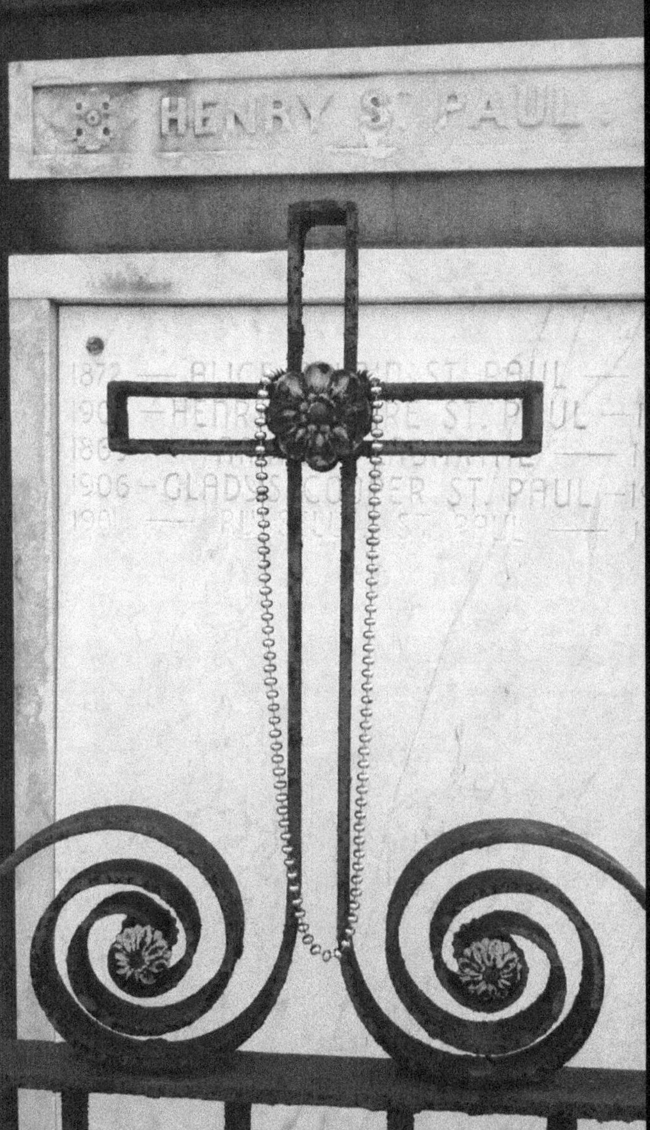

HENRY ST. PAUL
1872 — ALICE ??? ST. PAUL
190? — HENRI ??RE ST. PAUL
186? — ???
1906 — GLADYS COOPER ST. PAUL
190? — ??? ST. PAUL

ALLEY

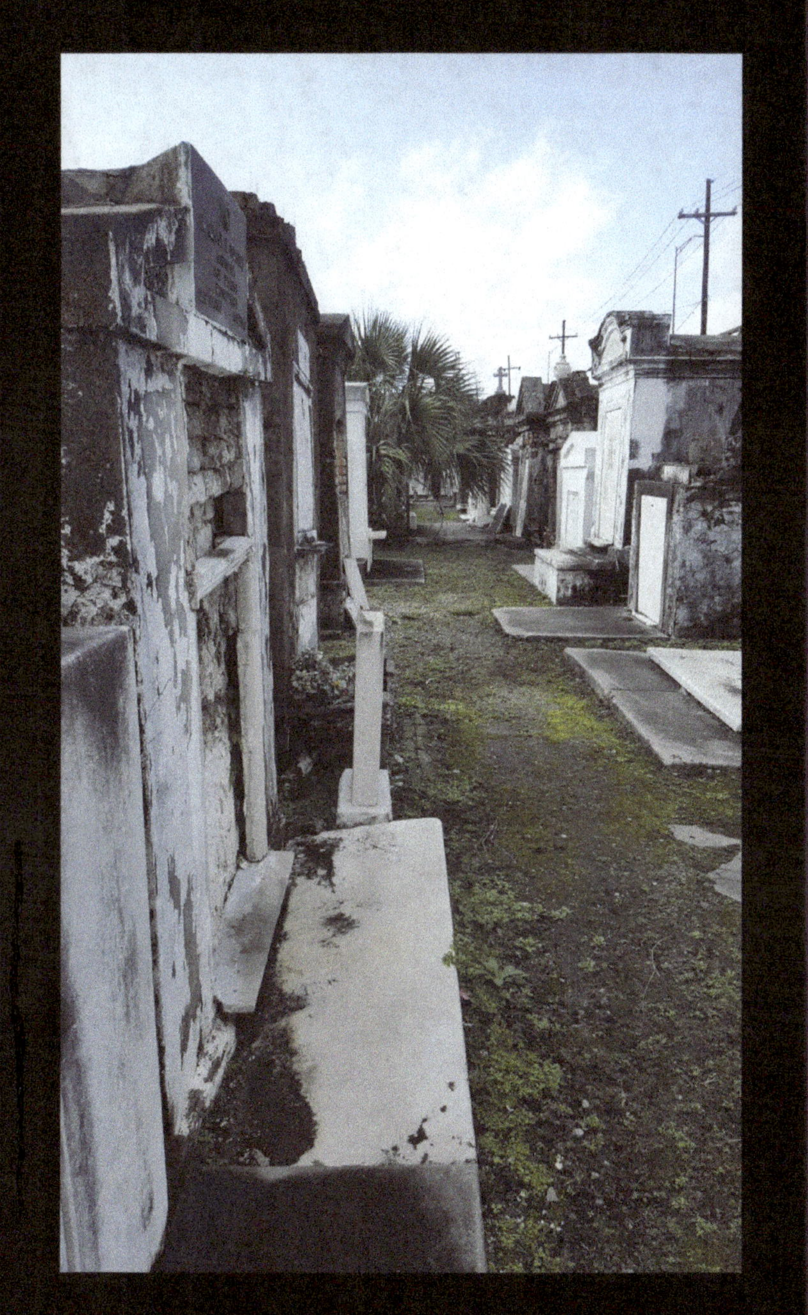

AMMONITES

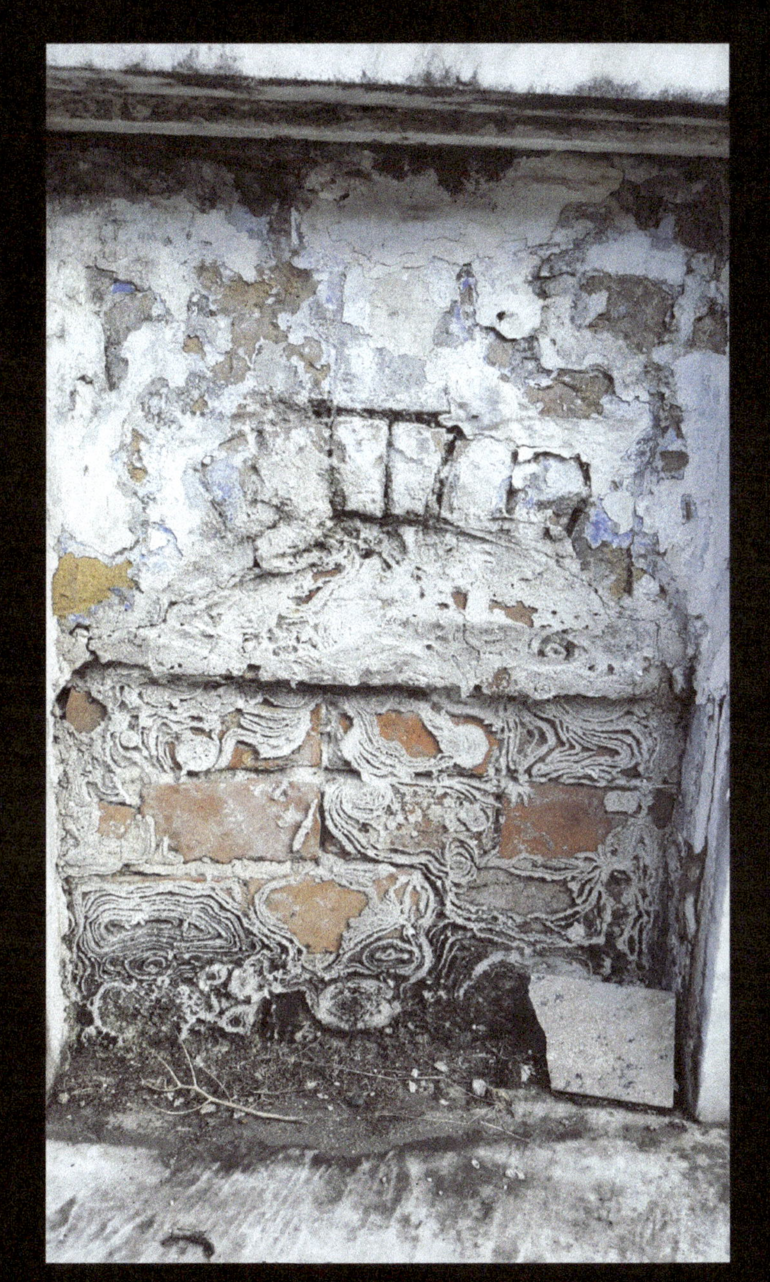

OBELISKS

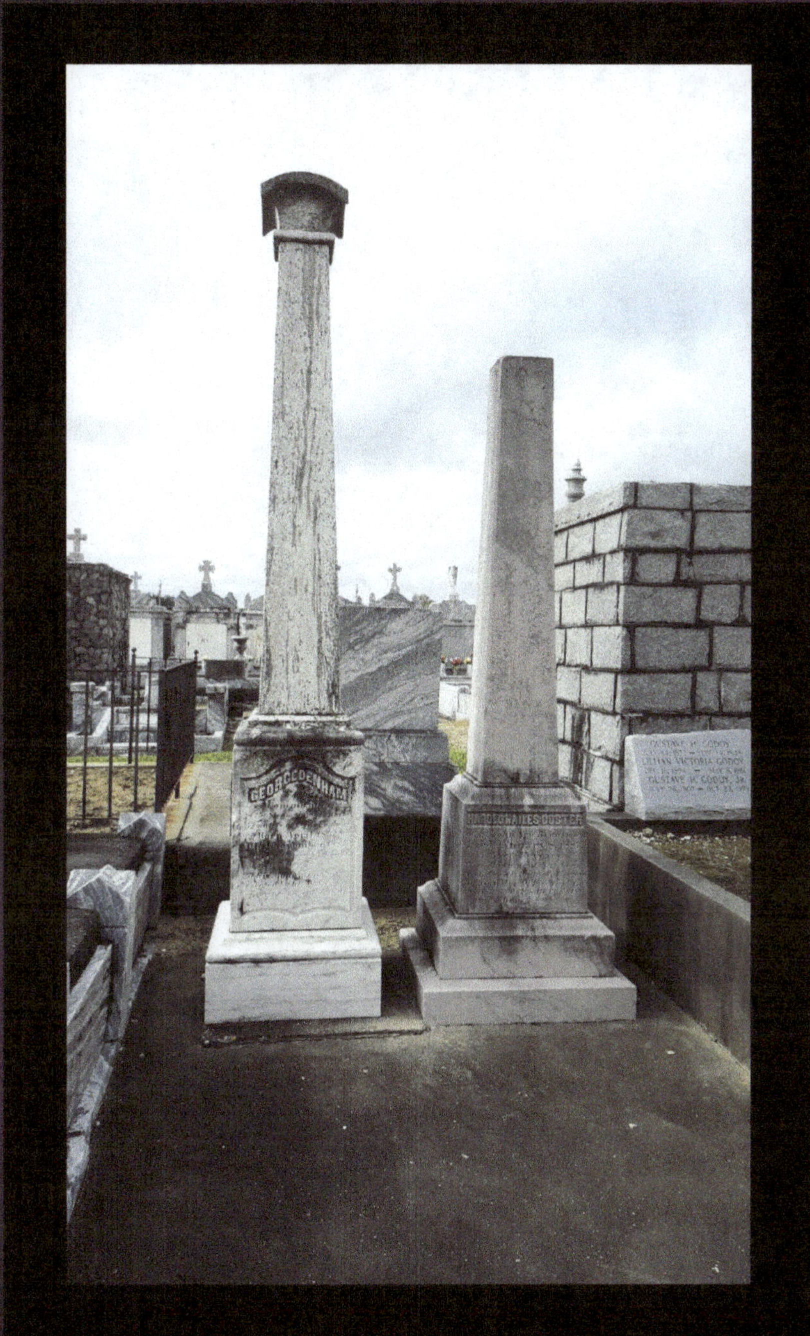
GEORGE DENHAM
CHARLES COSTER
GUSTAVE M. GODOY
LILLIAN VICTORIA GODOY
GUSTAVE M. GODOY, JR.

STEP UP,
REVEREND CONRAD

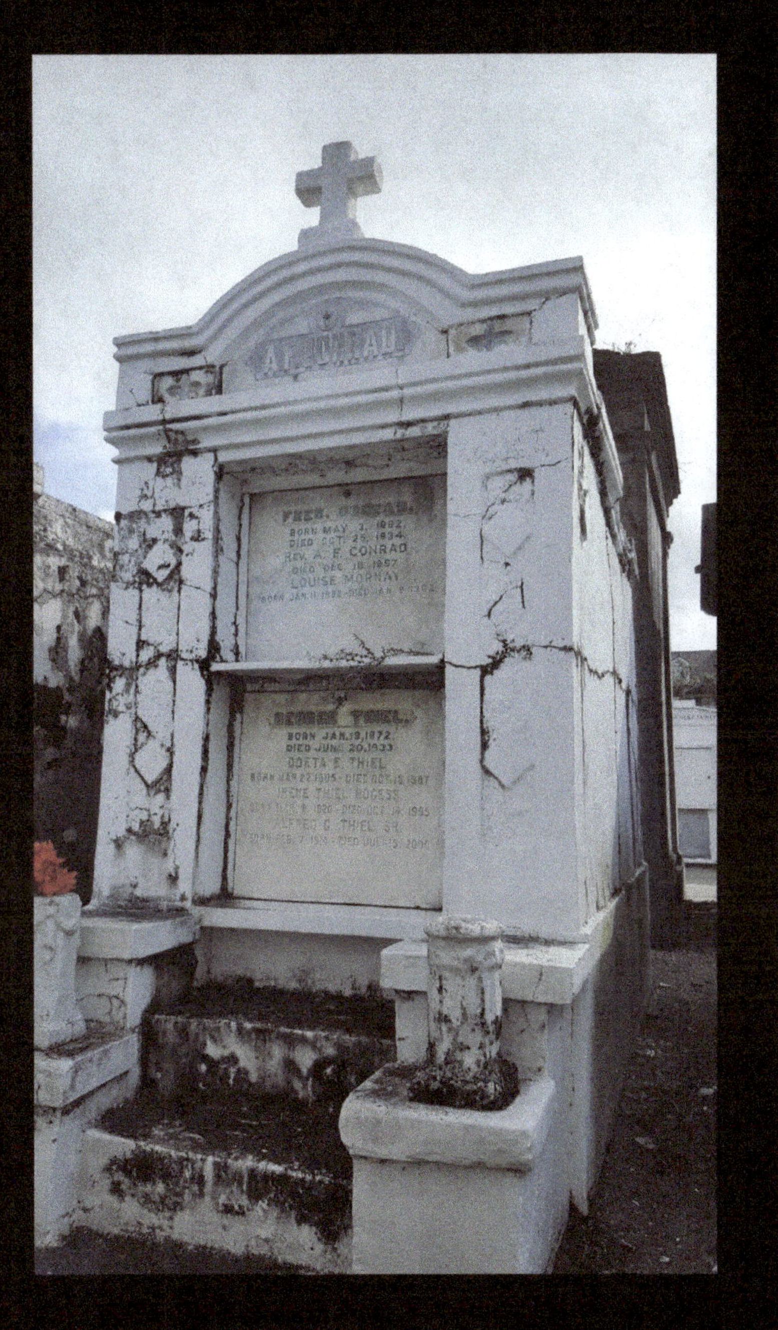
FRED. CONRAD.
BORN MAY 1, 1882.
DIED OCT. 25, 1934.
REV. A. F. CONRAD
DIED DEC. 18, 1957
LOUISE MORNAY
BORN JAN. 11, 1882 DIED JAN. 9, 1962
GEORGE THIEL.
BORN JAN. 19, 1872.
DIED JUNE 20, 1933
DORTA E. THIEL
BORN MAR 22 1905 DIED NOV 19 1987
IRENE THIEL BOGESS
BORN MAR 9, 1920 DIED OCT 18, 1995
ALFRED G. THIEL SR.
BORN FEB 7, 1923 DIED JULY 15, 2014

HADES

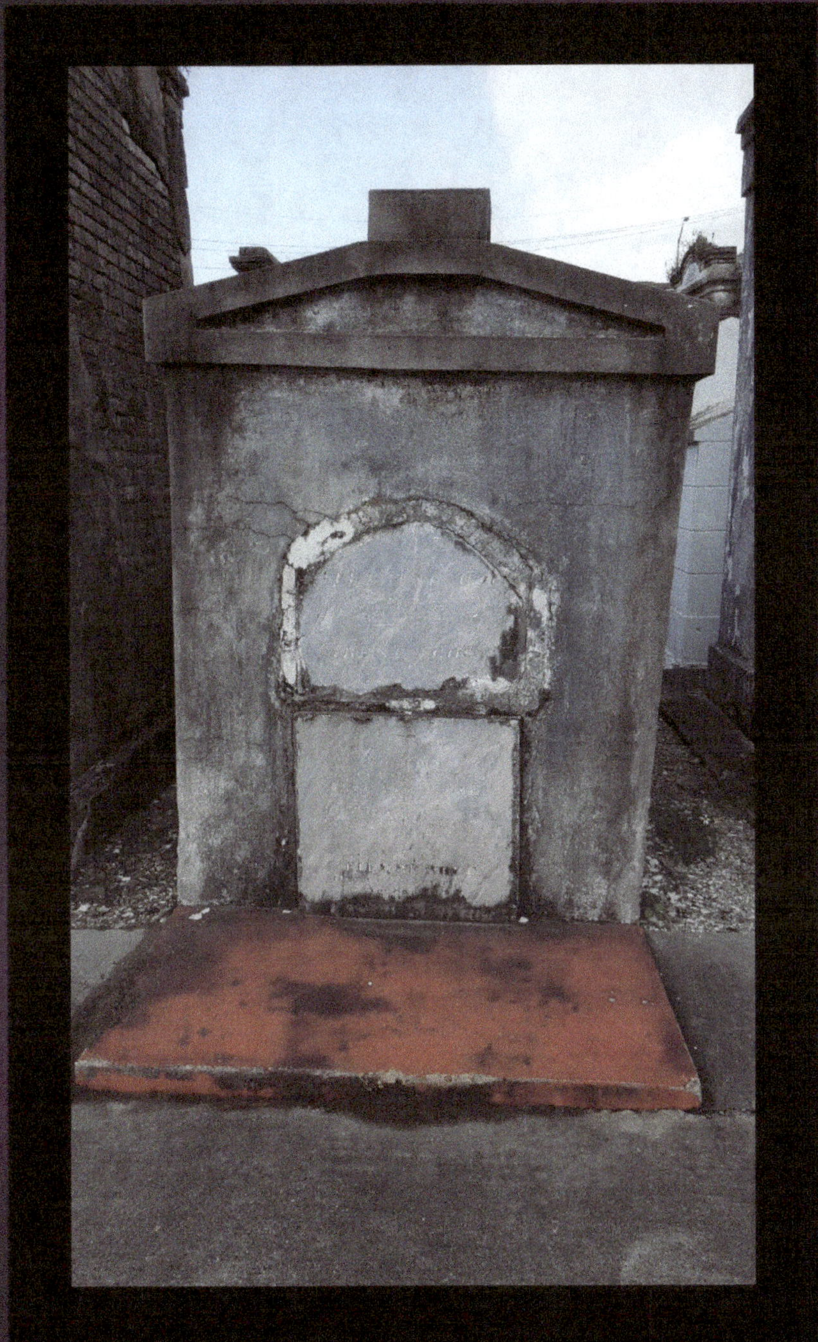

TENEMENT

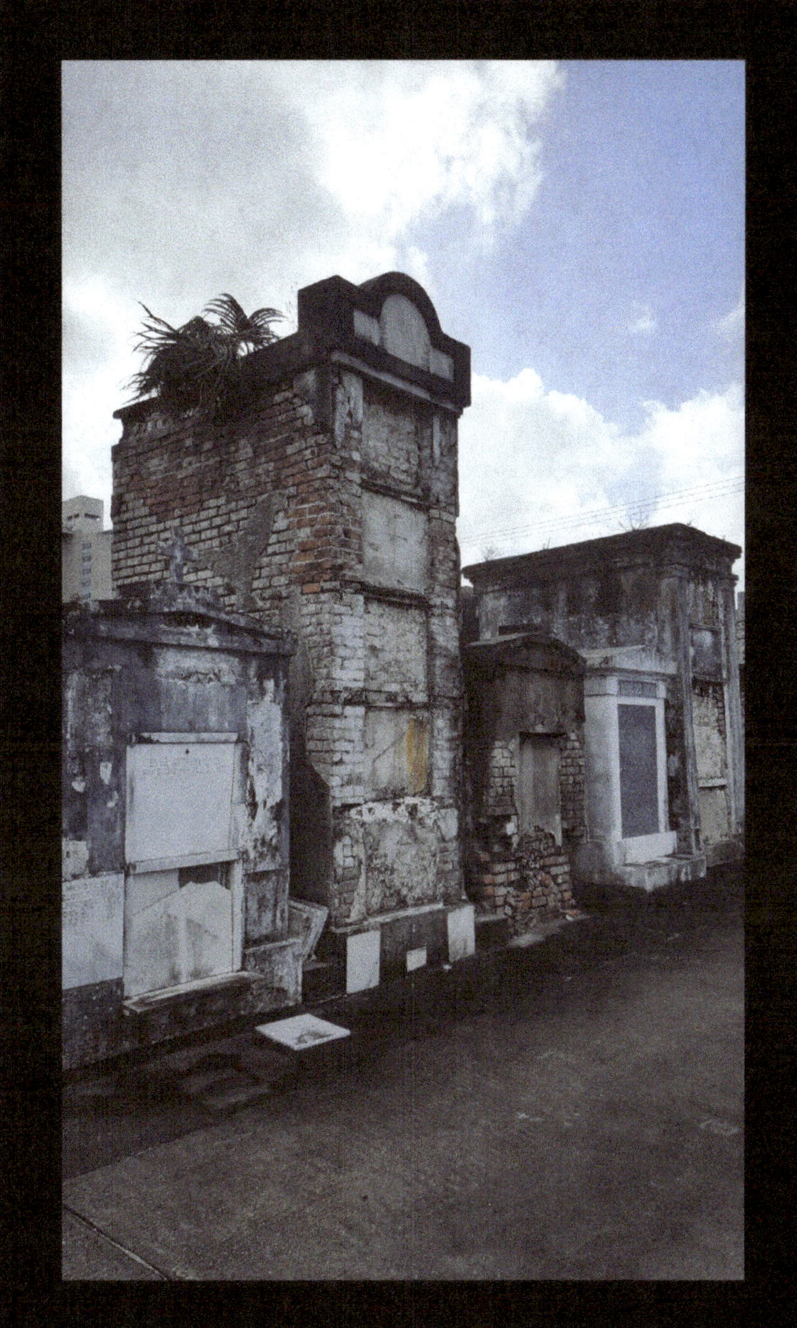

WHITE WITH PICKET FENCE

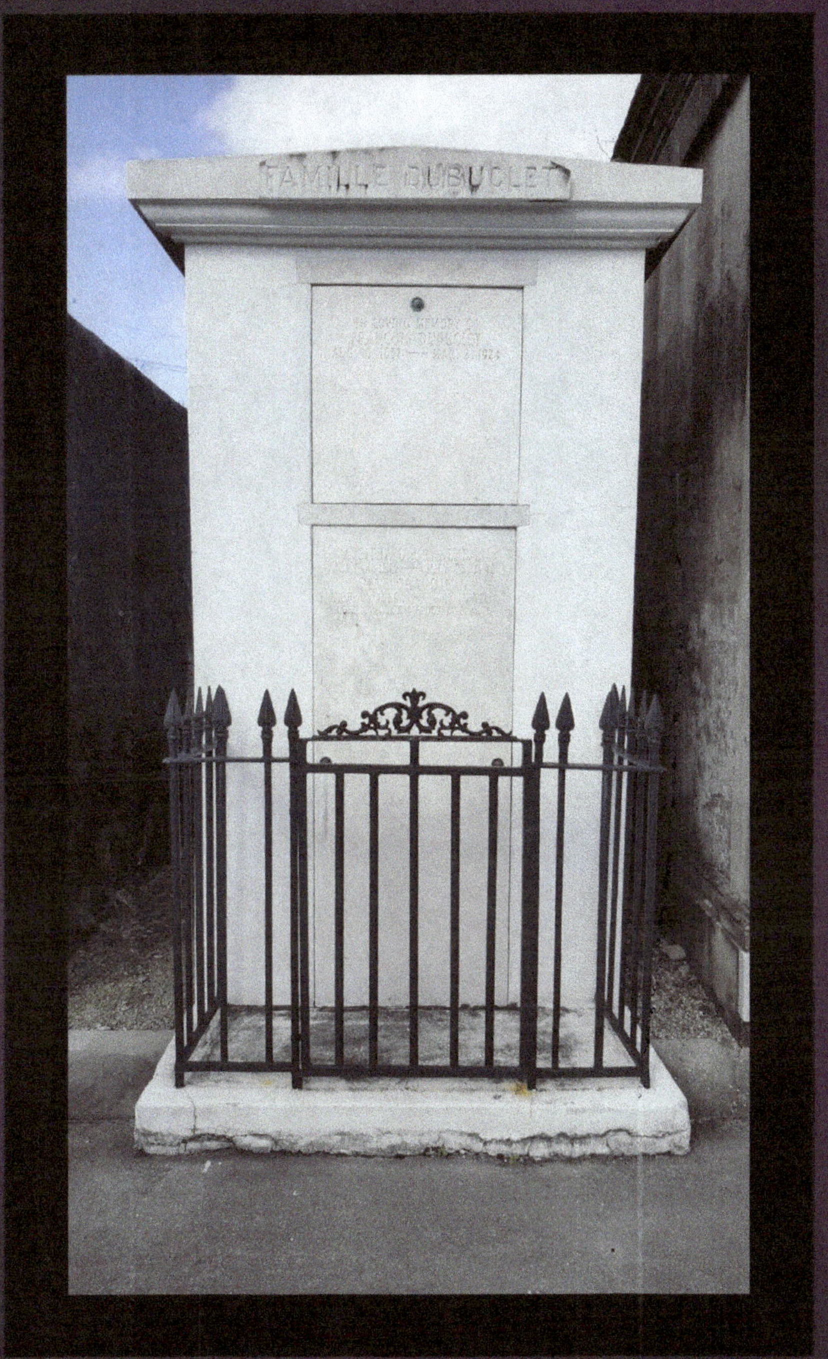
FAMILLE DUBUCLET

METAMORPHIC

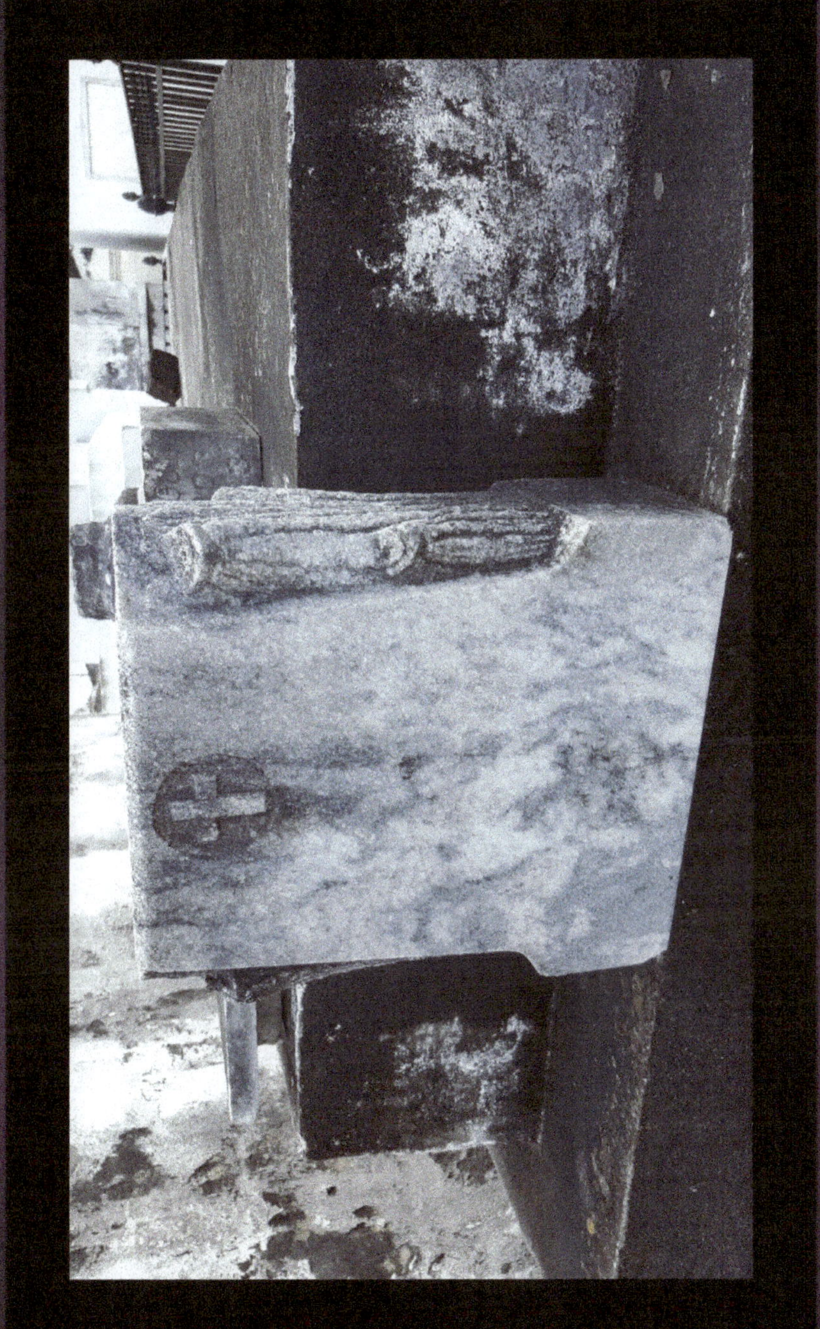

GHOST RISING

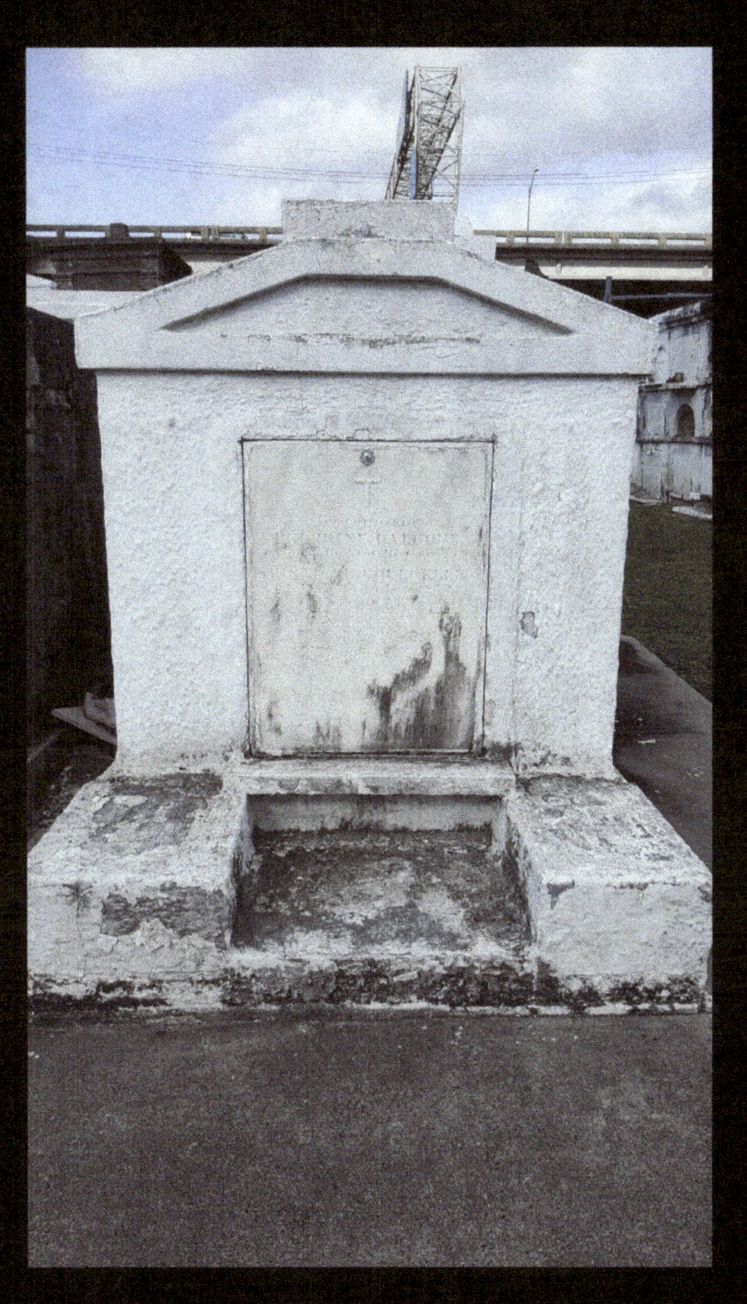

ALL TUCKED IN

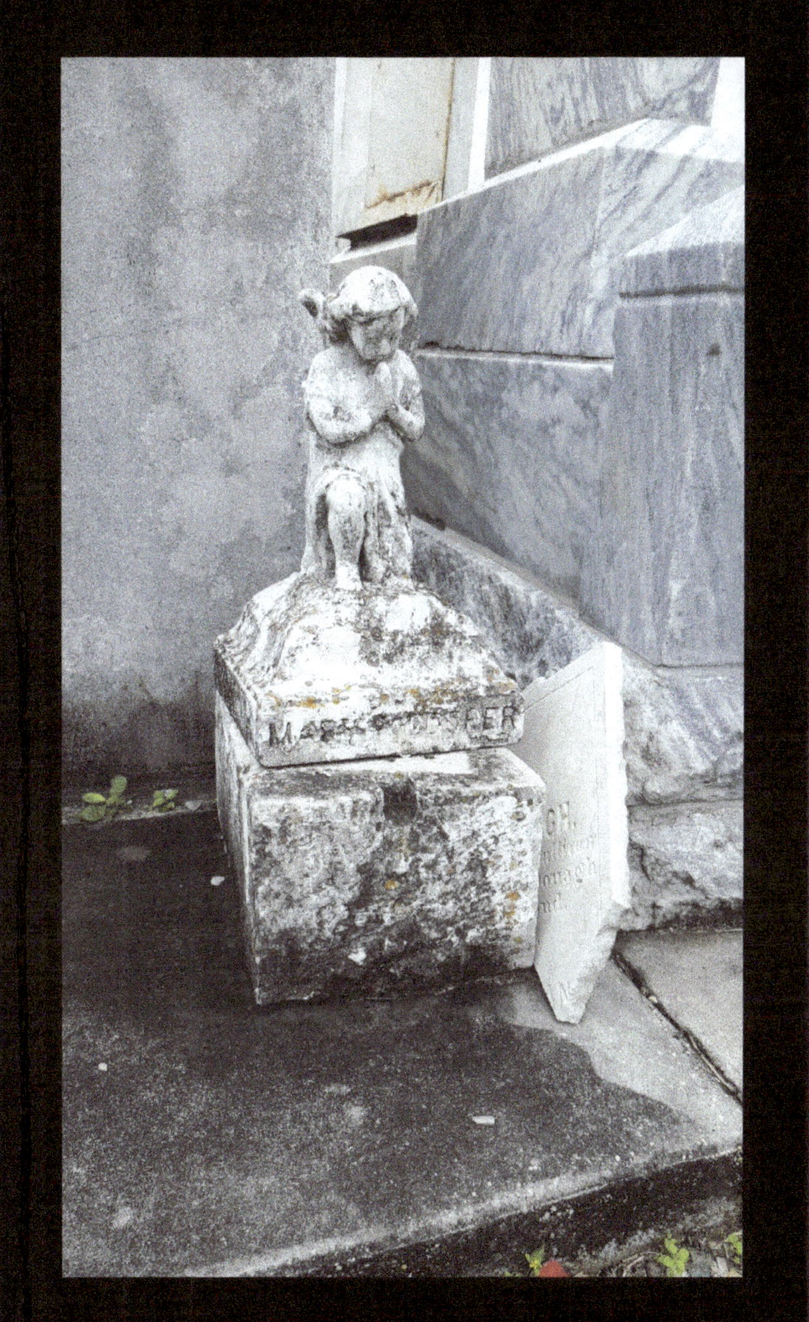

MARY GANUCHER

SKYLINE

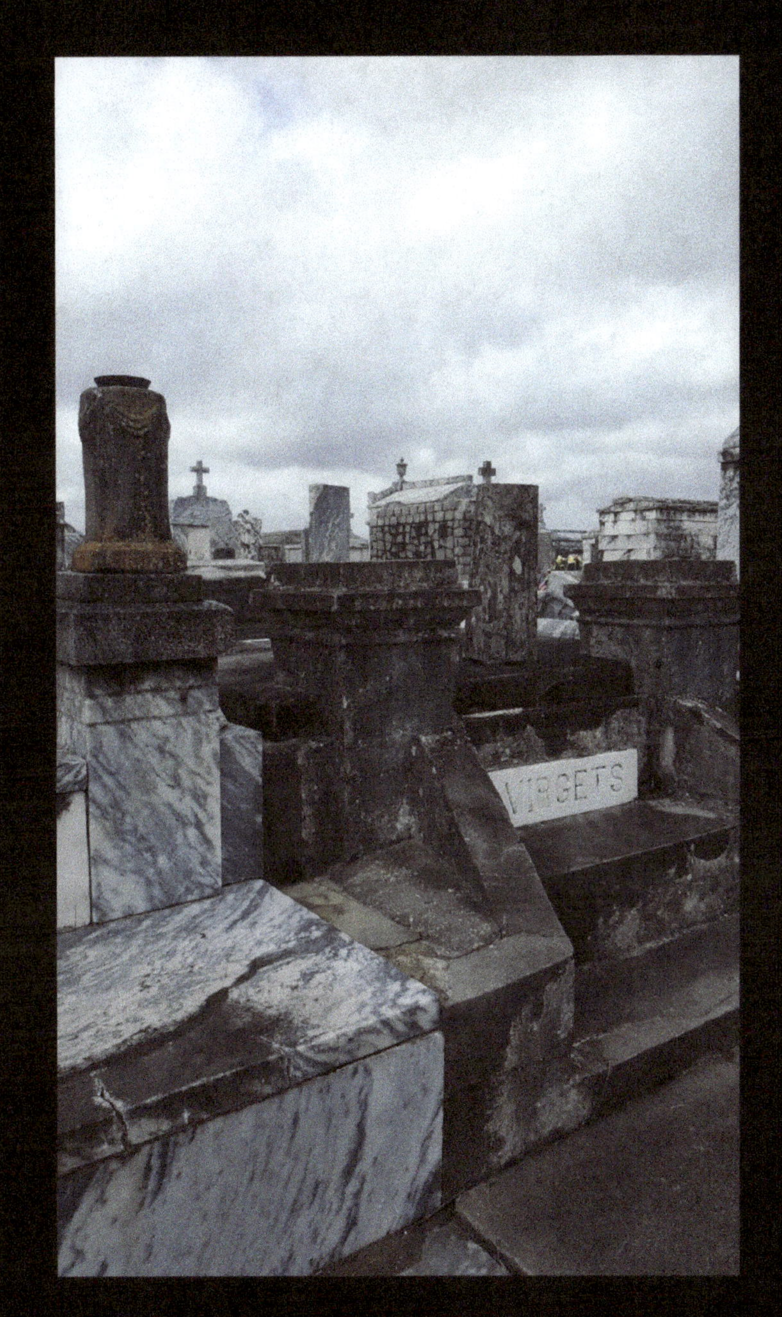
VIRGETS

PLANTER

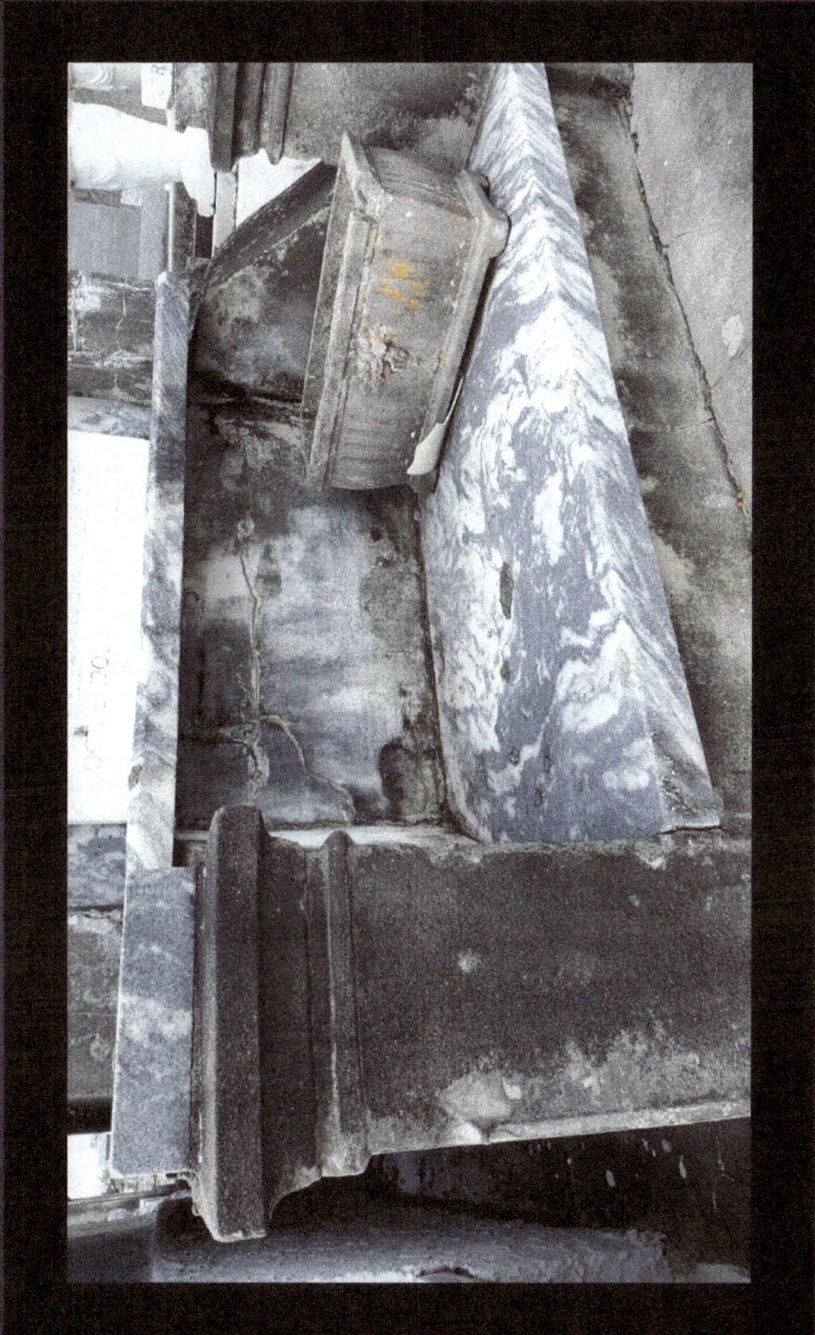

MOSSY LANE

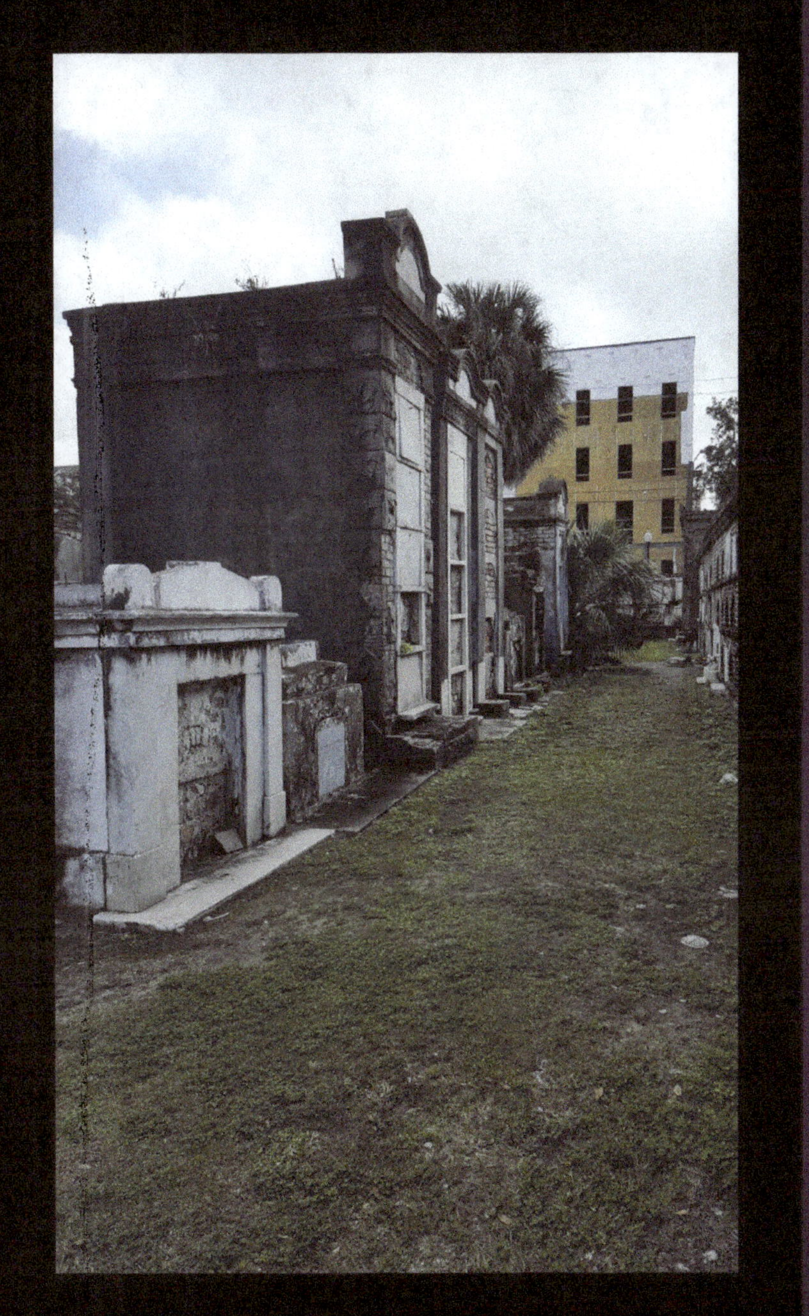

LANCE TIPS

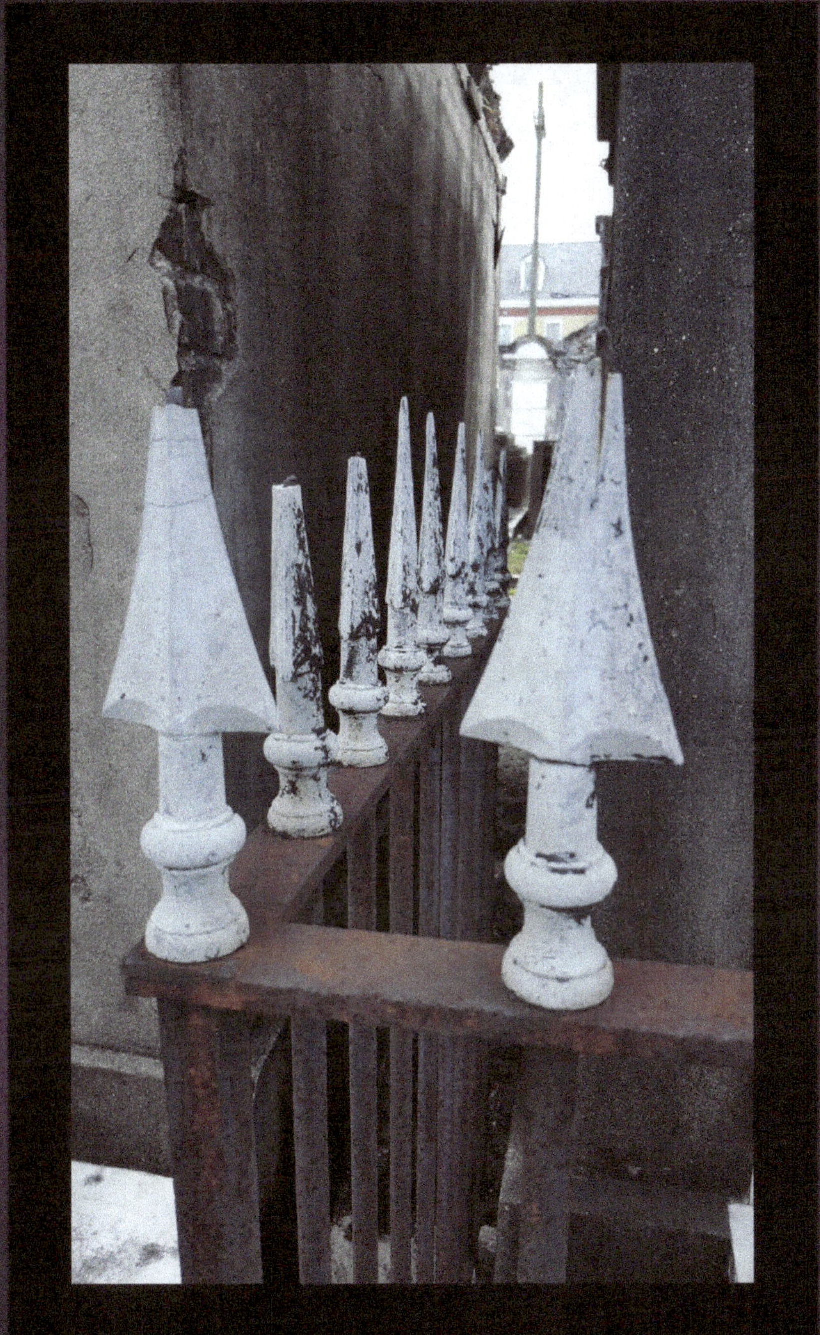

RISING

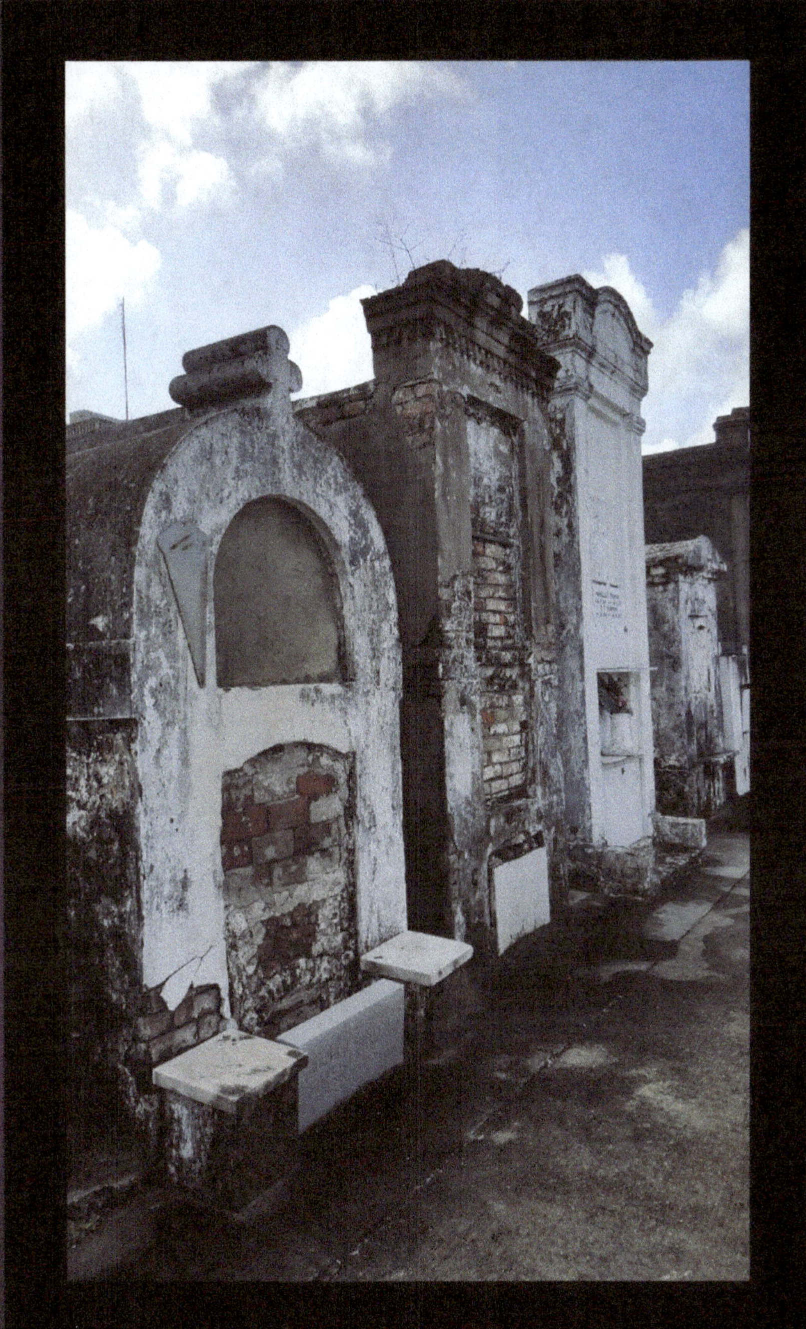

BACKYARD

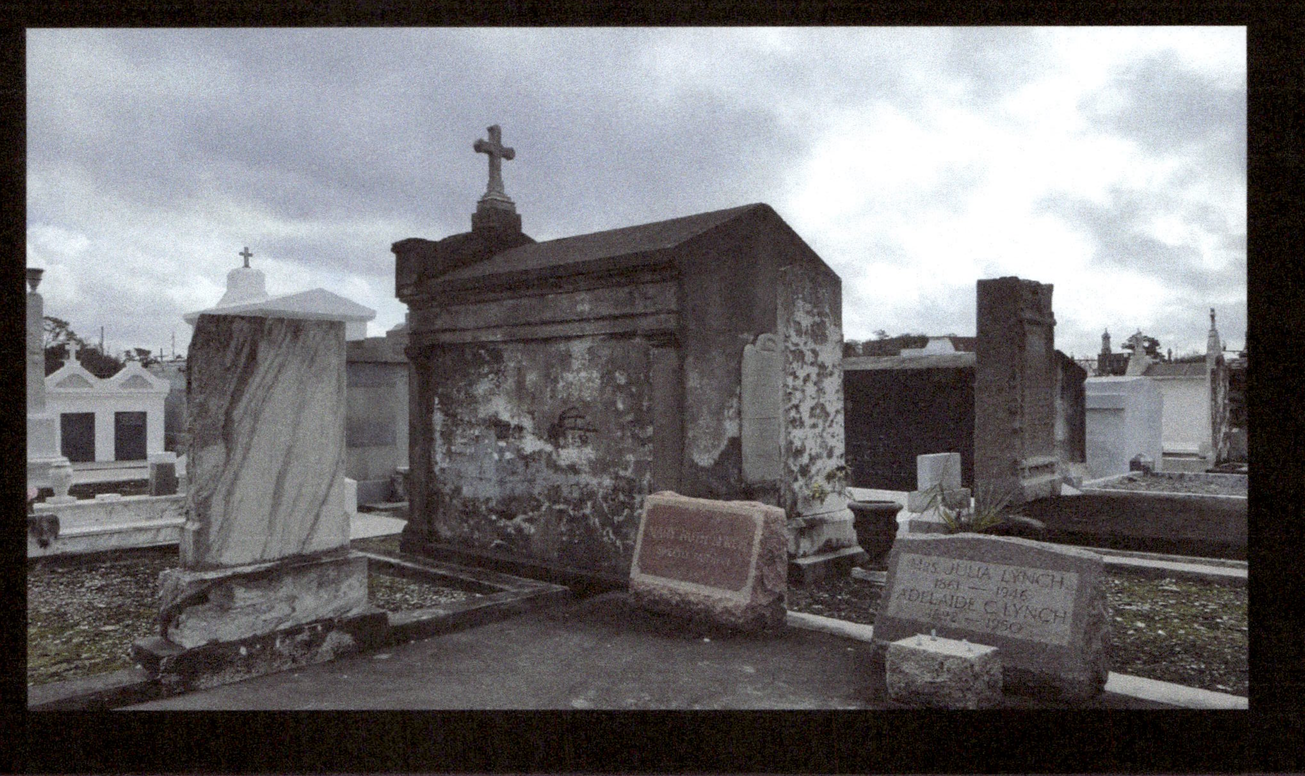

MRS JULIA LYNCH
1841 — 1946
ADELAIDE C LYNCH
1872 — 1950

About the Author

Laine Cunningham is an award-winning novelist whose career takes her around the world for extended stays. She enjoys sharing these special times with readers through the Travel Photo Art series.

Novels by Laine Cunningham

The Family Made of Dust
Beloved
Reparation

Other Books by Laine Cunningham

Woman Alone
A Six-Month Journey Through the Australian Outback

The *Woman Alone* Companion Series

On the Wallaby Track
18,000 Miles
Fairy Bread and Bush Tucker
Amazing Australia

Seven Sisters
Spiritual Messages from Aboriginal Australia

Writing While Female or Black or Gay
Diverse Voices in Publishing

The Zen for Life Series

The Zen of Travel
The Zen of Gardening
Zen in the Stable
The Zen of Chocolate
The Zen of Dogs

The Wisdom for Life Series

The Wisdom of Puppies
The Wisdom of Babies
The Wisdom of Weddings

The Travel Photo Art Series

Bikes of Berlin
Necropolises of New Orleans I & II
Ruins of Rome
Ancients of Assisi
Panoramas of Portugal

www.ingramcontent.com/pod-product-compliance
Lightning Source LLC
Chambersburg PA
CBHW061045050726
47592CB00004B/1602